Microsoft Orleans for Developers

Build Cloud-Native, High-Scale, Distributed Systems in .NET Using Orleans

Richard Astbury

Apress®

Microsoft Orleans for Developers: Build Cloud-Native, High-Scale, Distributed Systems in .NET Using Orleans

Richard Astbury
Woodbridge, UK

ISBN-13 (pbk): 978-1-4842-8166-6   ISBN-13 (electronic): 978-1-4842-8167-3
https://doi.org/10.1007/978-1-4842-8167-3

Managing Director, Apress Media LLC: Welmoed Spahr
Acquisitions Editor: Joan Murray
Development Editor: Laura Berendson
Coordinating Editor: Jill Balzano

Cover image designed by Freepik (www.freepik.com)

Distributed to the book trade worldwide by Springer Science+Business Media LLC, 1 New York Plaza, Suite 4600, New York, NY 10004. Phone 1-800-SPRINGER, fax (201) 348-4505, e-mail orders-ny@springer-sbm. com, or visit www.springeronline.com. Apress Media, LLC is a California LLC and the sole member (owner) is Springer Science + Business Media Finance Inc (SSBM Finance Inc). SSBM Finance Inc is a **Delaware** corporation.

For information on translations, please e-mail booktranslations@springernature.com; for reprint, paperback, or audio rights, please e-mail bookpermissions@springernature.com.

Apress titles may be purchased in bulk for academic, corporate, or promotional use. eBook versions and licenses are also available for most titles. For more information, reference our Print and eBook Bulk Sales web page at http://www.apress.com/bulk-sales.

Any source code or other supplementary material referenced by the author in this book is available to readers on GitHub.

Printed on acid-free paper

This book is dedicated to all those who have contributed to the Orleans community.

Table of Contents

About the Author

Richard Astbury works at Microsoft UK, helping software teams build software systems to run in the cloud. Richard is a former Microsoft MVP for Windows Azure. He is often found developing open source software in C# and Node.js, navigating the river on his paddle board, and riding his bike. He lives in rural Suffolk, UK, with his wife, three children, and golden retriever.

About the Technical Reviewer

Sergey Bykov is one of the creators of Orleans and a long-time lead of the project since its inception within Microsoft Research. During his nearly 20 years at Microsoft, he has worked on servers, embedded systems, online and gaming services. His passion has always been about providing tools and frameworks for software engineers, to help them build better, faster, more reliable and scalable systems and applications with less effort. He continues to follow that passion, now at Temporal Technologies.

You can read Sergey's blog at `https://dev.to/sergeybykov` and follow him on Twitter @sergeybykov.

Introduction

Welcome!

This book aims to help the experienced dotnet developer understand what Orleans is, what problems it solves, and how to get started with an Orleans project. No prior knowledge of distributed systems is required, but it is useful to have a good grasp of C#, ASP.NET Core, and unit testing.

The first two chapters provide a brief history and backstory, helping you understand where Orleans began and the core concepts, namely, Grains and Silos.

The main body of the book starts with a "Hello World" example and then explores several of the features of Orleans by building more functionality into this application. This helps us to understand the functionality of Orleans by taking practical steps and building something that's a, sort of, real system.

I have included a couple of chapters on more advanced features, including optimizations. I don't attempt to add all of these to the sample application, and instead explain how they're used and the problems they solve.

Software is built by people, and it was important to me to include some interviews in this book from people who are/were in the core team as well as the community. I hope you enjoy reading their perspectives.

Orleans is a great fit for some really interesting challenges, particularly around high-scale, real-time systems, but it doesn't fit every problem. Part of being an experienced developer is knowing the best tool to use for a given problem. My hope is that this book will help you develop your intuition, so when you have finished reading (however far you get!), you'll know an Orleans-shaped problem when you see one.

CHAPTER 1

Fundamentals

Microsoft Orleans is a free, open source framework built on Microsoft .NET, which provides the developer with a simple programming model enabling them to build software which can scale from a single machine to hundreds of servers.

You can think of Orleans as a distributed runtime, which runs software across a cluster of servers, treating them as a single address space. This allows the developer to build software which keeps lots of data in memory, by spreading objects across the cluster's shared memory space. This enables low-latency systems, where requests can be processed using data held in memory without deferring to a database. This allows the system to deal with a high volume of traffic.

Orleans is designed to support cloud-native applications, with elasticity and fault tolerance.

Orleans is a "batteries included" framework, which ships with many of the features required for distributed systems built in.

Motivation for Orleans

When I first started serious programming in the early 1990s, it was just me, my PC, and Turbo Pascal 7. The terrible software I wrote just ran on a single machine, an IBM PS/2 8086, which had a single CPU core and no network.

Fast-forward to the present day and the progress made in computer hardware is astonishing. Computers now have multiple cores, with 440 being the current state of the art. Cloud computing provides us with near instant rental to computers with per-minute billing, almost limitless horizontal scalability, and accessible to anyone via a ubiquitous global network – the Internet.

© Richard Astbury 2022
R. Astbury, *Microsoft Orleans for Developers*, https://doi.org/10.1007/978-1-4842-8167-3_1

While programming languages have also evolved, most mainstream languages are still generally focused on running a sequence of instructions on a single computer. Some languages' runtimes don't even have support for multithreading and distributing work across multiple cores.

In order to satisfy the requirements of real-time web applications and IoT gateways, developers are required to build systems that can deal with high volumes of traffic, handle hardware failure, and do this with elasticity to optimize for cost. We need to make efficient use of the hardware, which means running code efficiently on multicore computers, horizontally scaled in the cloud.

I think most experienced developers would agree that programming concurrent or distributed systems is hard. Bugs in concurrent code, such as race conditions, are sometimes hard to detect, to replicate, to debug, and to test. Software that runs across networks must respond to transient outage and delays, which are common in a cloud environment. The developer will often have to consider eventual consistency or reconciling state mutations across multiple nodes.

Languages have emerged that certainly help the developer to build concurrent and networked software, with reference to Go and Rust in particular, but my opinion is that while these languages offer constructs and safety for concurrent programming, they don't provide a finished solution for a developer to build software that's distributed by default.

In response to these challenges, the design I see the majority of developers take is to make application code stateless and use the database to handle concurrency using transactions and optimistic locking. This allows horizontal scalability of the application server. The servers do not cooperate or communicate between each other, as every state mutation is performed by the database. This requires the web server to gather the required records from the database to respond to each request. This is an excellent solution, which has been proven to work countless times. However, there are a couple of problems that can emerge:

1. The database can become a performance bottleneck, and while databases can be scaled vertically (i.e., upgrade the hardware), you will eventually reach a limit. Some databases can be horizontally scaled. However, this often comes with a loss in some guarantees, such as eventual consistency rather than strong consistency.

2. The system can become slow, as state from the database must be loaded in order to serve the request. This is often addressed with an in-memory cache, to hold regularly accessed data in RAM, which provides a faster means of access. This now means we have state in two places, and cache invalidation can become challenging. It also feels like a band-aid over the problem rather than fixing it fundamentally.

Orleans addresses these challenges by thinking about the problem in a different way. Instead of having an external cache to store data in memory, it provides a means to maintain a set of current objects in memory. These objects not only encapsulate state but also logic.

Another way to think about this is that rather than fetching the data needed to service a request (from an external database or cache), the request is directed to the place where the data is held in memory. That way, the object has the ability to fulfill the request without the need to load data from an external system.

This has a nice symmetry to the original "big data" thinking, where map-reduce functions are scheduled on servers holding the data files, rather than loading data into a central data warehouse.

To execute code on one of the objects in Orleans, you send a message to it. The objects can call further objects in a call chain if required.

Logic inside an object is subject to a turn-based concurrency model. This means that no two requests are processed simultaneously, removing the need for us to lock state variables or data structures for thread safety.

Orleans lifts a few concepts out of the database, such as transactions, which allows you to use an underlying data store with a fairly limited set of guarantees, but provides ACID compliance at the application level.

Orleans also provides a simple programming model, making it accessible to a broader population of developers without experience in building distributed systems.

Brief History of Orleans

Orleans started as an internal project in Microsoft Research. The launch of Microsoft Azure prompted an exploration into new ways of building software to be cloud native.

The team responsible for building the cloud software infrastructure to support the *Halo 4* game selected Orleans. Orleans was selected for its simple programming model and ability to support the high traffic volumes predicted for the launch of the game.

After gaining traction with other teams within Microsoft, Orleans was made accessible via a Technology Access Program to selected parties outside Microsoft. This culminated in the open sourcing of Orleans as it reached version 1.0.0 in early 2015.

Orleans saw high community engagement which was surprising not only because Orleans was a fairly niche project, does not have a marketing budget, and is technically quite challenging to approach as a contributor.

Orleans continues to have a core team supported by Microsoft and an engaged community which regularly contributes to the code base, a contrib organization on GitHub, online meetups, and an active discord server.

Orleans Timeline

- Early 2009: Orleans project starts

- Late 2011: Orleans used by internal teams

- November 2012: *Halo 4* released

- August 2013: Technology Access Program opened for external users to preview Orleans

- March 2014: "Orleans: Distributed Virtual Actors for Programmability and Scalability" paper released

- April 2014: Public preview released on CodePlex

- January 2015: Orleans open sourced on GitHub

- February 2015: Orleans v1.0.0 released

- March 2018: Orleans v2.0.0 released

- October 2019: Orleans v3.0.0 released

Use Cases

Orleans does not fit every use case perfectly. As with every technology, a careful selection should be made based on the requirements of the system and the skillset of the development team.

Orleans is a great fit for these situations:

- Modeling independent entities with partitionable state, such as devices, users, or sessions.

- Low latency is a critical factor.

- A high or variable traffic volume, requiring high scale/scalability.

- High availability.

- A high degree of parallelism is required.

- The team has .NET experience (C# or F#).

- Data streaming or reactive programming.

Orleans does not fit these requirements:

- Running queries over large data sets (i.e., map/reduce or search).

- CPU-intensive algorithms such as video encoding.

Orleans could be run in conjunction with other systems to provide this kind of functionality, such as using SQL Server to provide aggregate queries, but there are no native features in Orleans to support these kinds of workloads.

There are numerous scenarios where Orleans fits well:

- Online gaming, such as connecting players to games and exchanging in-game data

- Chat rooms and messaging

- Internet of Things

- Ingestion of telemetry

- Stock/gambling where real-time valuation/risk is modeled

- Event-based applications, such as web socket connected web pages

Architectures

System architecture is a hot topic, with a current industry fashion to move away from monolithic software systems and adopt microservices.

When asked how Orleans fits into this landscape, the answer is simple. Orleans is an application framework that can be considered as a service within a microservice environment, or it could be a stand-alone monolith. I have seen people consider it a "nanoservices" or "megalith" architecture, whereby it forms the runtime for lots of small services or for multiple applications.

However you think about it, or whatever your architectural preference, you can use Orleans as an application runtime which can scale from a single docker container to hundreds of servers; it's up to you how you build the rest of the system.

Cloud

It is worth mentioning that while Orleans was designed for the cloud, in particular Microsoft Azure, it is by no means bound to the cloud. Orleans can be run anywhere where .NET Core can run, which includes Windows, Linux, or containers. There is library support for AWS, GCP, and Azure, and it can be hosted just as easily on-premises.

Orleans is extensible by design, so if a service doesn't have an adaptor developed for it, either by the core team or the community, there is nothing stopping you from developing your own.

Summary

We start the book by looking at the challenges facing the modern software developer and how Orleans is a rethink to the traditional approach for building software, by co-locating state and logic into an object which is hosted on a cluster of servers that are all connected and act as a single runtime.

In the next chapter, we'll dig into the programming constructs of Orleans and get into some of the detail.

CHAPTER 2

Grains and Silos

In this chapter, we will dig into the fundamental components of Orleans: Grains and Silos.

Grains

In the previous chapter, we learnt that Orleans keeps objects in memory, these objects have both state and logic, and the system routes requests to them based on their identity. In Orleans, we call this object a "Grains." This is analogous to a grains of wheat, as we think of these objects as small and in abundance.

The properties of a grains are as follows:

- Grains have an identity.

- Only a single instance of a grains will be activated for a given identity and grains type. This is guaranteed for periods when the cluster is not undergoing a network failure.

- Orleans creates instances of grains when required (just in time).

- Orleans garbage collects grains that have stopped receiving messages.

- Grains code is executed with turn-based concurrency. This means the grains processes one request at a time, by default, and requests are queued until the grains is ready.

We will explore these properties in more detail in this chapter and throughout the rest of the book.

© Richard Astbury 2022
R. Astbury, *Microsoft Orleans for Developers*, https://doi.org/10.1007/978-1-4842-8167-3_2

Note   Grains prefer availability over consistency. This means that if the network is undergoing a partition or similar kind of failure and Orleans thinks a node cannot be reached, it may permit multiple activations of a grains. When a node discovers it has been evicted from the cluster, the duplicate grains instances are automatically disposed of.

Grains are defined using an interface, for example:

```
public interface IExampleGrain : IGrainWithStringKey
{
  Task<string> SayHello(string name);
}
```

Note   In this book, all code samples are provided in C#. However, Orleans also supports F#, and it's entirely the preference of the developer which to use.

Grains interfaces define asynchronous methods (methods that return a Task). You could think of these methods as the signatures of messages that the grains can receive and respond with. In this case, the "SayHello" message accepts a string and returns a string.

The interface inherits the IGrainWithStringKey interface, provided by Orleans, which indicates that a string is used as the identity for this grains. We will explore identity further on in this chapter.

A Grains is a class that implements the interface, and also the Grain base class provided by Orleans.

```
public class ExampleGrain : Grain, IExampleGrain
{
  public Task<string> SayHello(string name)
  {
    return Task.FromResult($"Hello, {name}");
  }
}
```

To call the grains we use a client object, we'll see later on in the book how we get a reference to the client object, but for now that's not important.

```
var grain = client.GetGrain<IExampleGrain>("grain123");
var result = await grain.SayHello("World");
// returns "Hello, World"
```

Grains Identity

A grain's identity can be a string, integer, GUID, or a combination of integer + string or GUID + string. This identity works in a similar way to a primary key for a database record, allowing separate processes to refer to the same grains.

The grains can read its identity, as this may be a useful value when referring to data required from other systems. For example, the identity could be a serial number or a username.

Identities are scoped to the grain's interface type, so two different grains types can have the same value for identity, and will be treated as completely different grains.

Grains Life Cycle

Grains do not need to be explicitly created, but instead are created when they are sent a message.

From the caller's perspective, the grains are always there; it's just a matter of whether they are currently in memory or not. This makes them "virtual," and we use the term "activate" rather than "create" to acknowledge this.

Grains remain active after the initial call to them is made. This allows subsequent calls to be processed using the internal state that the grains maintains in memory. Keeping the right data in memory means we can minimize the calls to external data stores or systems, and allows grains to respond quickly and efficiently to requests.

Orleans will deactivate idle grains activations that are no longer receiving messages, i.e., they are no longer actively in use. This frees up resources for new activations. By default, this idle time is 2 hours, but this is configurable as a global setting or on a per-grains basis.

A grains can easily be reactivated as required; from the caller's perspective, it's always available.

It can be helpful to think of grains as always existing, but they can be moved in and out of a working set based on demand, automatically.

A grains has some degree of control over life cycle behavior and can request immediate deactivation or prolong its activation. In most use cases, you can rely on the runtime doing the right thing so you won't need to manipulate the lifetime.

Turn-Based Concurrency

Grains have a turn-based concurrency model. This means that a given activation will only process one message at a time. If multiple messages arrive at a grains, they are queued (in memory).

By default, the grains will only process the next message when the current message has completely finished, even when the grains is awaiting an external task to complete. This behavior can be changed to allow interleaving of calls, so a grains can process a message while it is awaiting. If you enable this, you may see side effects such as the grain's internal state changing while a method is awaiting an external task, so care must be taken.

More about how to configure this behavior can be found in Chapter 14.

Message Delivery Guarantees

Distributed systems can never provide "exactly once" message delivery. You can either have "at most once" or "at least once." By default, Orleans is "at most once."

When sending a message to a grains, it will either succeed, or an exception will be thrown. This could be due to application logic in the grains, bad configuration in Orleans, or a transient runtime error such as a failure in the network. Calls that exceed a timeout period are cancelled, and an error is thrown.

Note   Note that the default timeout period is 30 seconds, but this is a configurable settings, but it's not intended for grains to handle long-running requests.

In the case of a transient runtime error, it's impossible to tell whether the grains received the message or not and whether the data was stored in a persistent store, as the fault could have occurred before or after the application logic. For this reason, Orleans is configured to never retry message delivery. Retying could lead to an undesirable outcome, such as a bank balance being credited twice.

If we are able to make messages idempotent, that is, that there are no unwanted side effects with multiple delivery, then we can add automatic retry in application logic, or we can configure Orleans to automatically retry.

Virtual Actors?

With the 2014 paper, the Orleans team introduced a new concept, the "virtual actor" (`www.microsoft.com/en-us/research/publication/orleans-distributed-virtual-actors-for-programmability-and-scalability/`).

To understand what a virtual actor is, we must first understand what we mean by an "actor."

The paper by Hewitt et al. (1973) describes an actor-based system, where an actor is "a programming primitive that can respond to messages, make local decisions, create more actors, send more messages, and determine how to respond to the next message received."

To summarize, it means actors have the following properties:

- They respond to messages, which suggests an asynchronous nature.

- They make local decisions, which means they have some logic.

- They can create more actors and send messages.

- They determine how to respond to the next message received, which implies they have some internal state that can mutate over time.

Since then, several actor systems have been developed, including Erlang and Akka. These systems generally have one-way messaging and supervision trees.

The supervision tree is a key difference with Orleans. Conventional actors are explicitly created by a supervising actor. This supervisor controls the life cycle of its children, restarting them if they encounter an error. Supervisors are also supervised, and so on until a tree structure is formed, with the main program process at the top level.

Orleans has no need for these supervision trees because the runtime itself activates and deactivates grains based on demand. But this has caused some confusion among developers accustomed to supervision trees being a regular feature of actor-based systems.

The Orleans team have reduced their emphasis on the actor word as it hasn't been a useful way to describe the system to developers. If you know what an actor is already, you have preconceived ideas about what an actor should be which then makes Orleans confusing to understand. If you haven't heard of the actor model before, then the term is of no use anyway! In this book, I will always call them Grains.

Silos

Following the analogy of Grains as tiny seeds, the Silos is the structure that contains them.

The Silos is the runtime that hosts the grains. The silos is delivered as a NuGet package and is configured and started by a host application in a very similar way to an ASP.NET web server.

A Silos could be hosted in a Windows Service or a console application. It could be packaged as a Docker Container and hosted in-cloud or on-premises.

You would typically host a single Silos per machine.

Silos do not have a public API and so must always be fronted by an API, such as an ASP. NET web server. The Web API could be co-hosted on the same server as the Silos, or they could be separated out into different servers, depending on the requirements of the system.

Silos are created with a few lines of code:

```
using var host = new HostBuilder()
  .UseOrleans(builder => /* provide configuration here */ )
  .Build();

await host.StartAsync();

// silo is running

await host.StopAsync();
```

Silos require two ports to be open. The gateway port (by default 30000) is used by clients to connect to the Silos. The Silos port (by default 11111) is used for Silos-to-Silos communication. Both ports use a custom TCP/IP-based protocol and are not designed to be consumed directly by third-party code. Instead, a Client connector, provided as part of Orleans, is used for calls into and between grains.

Neither port should be open to the public Internet; Orleans should always be hosted behind an API.

Silos share a distributed hash table which acts as the directory of where each of the grains is located. When a request from a client arrives at a Silos, if the Grains is not activated, it will forward the request to the correct Silos if necessary.

One advantage of co-hosting the ASP.NET Web API in the same process as the Silos is that the client can access the distributed hash table and look up the location of grains. This can reduce network hops.

The Scheduler

The scheduler is a custom TPL Task Scheduler which the Silos uses to execute the grains methods in response to messages.

When a message is received by the correct Silos, it creates a Task and enqueues it on a task scheduler specific to that grains activation (the Activation Task Scheduler).

When new messages arrive, the .NET thread pool invokes the Activation Task Scheduler which in turn invokes each enqueued Task.

The .NET thread pool is sized in accordance with the number of logical cores on the system. It is therefore important not to block a thread in grains code, as the thread pool will quickly be starved, and the Silos performance will suffer considerably.

Cluster Membership Protocol

Orleans Silos form a cluster, that is, a set of nodes that cooperate as a single system. Each Silos needs to know about the other members, when Silos join, leave, or have failed. Silos also need to share their IP addresses so they can send messages between each other.

To support these requirements, Orleans uses an external data store to hold cluster membership information. When a Silos starts, it writes its identity (which is a combination of IP address, port number, and the current timestamp) to the table.

Each Silos then monitors a number of the other Silos in the cluster, by sending them regular heartbeat messages on the Silos-to-Silos port. The Silos it chooses to monitor are calculated using a consistent hashing algorithm which ensures that every silos is monitored by multiple other silos.

If a Silos suspects that another Silos has failed, which could be a software failure, hardware failure, or network failure, it writes this as a suspicion to the membership table.

If a Silos receives a set number of suspicions within a given timeframe, the Silos is marked as dead and removed from the cluster's membership.

Silos regularly read the membership table, but silos will send a snapshot of the table to each other when membership changes to propagate this information quickly across the cluster.

If the membership table cannot be read, perhaps because of a temporary network failure, the Silos will continue to operate, but the cluster's membership will not change.

Orleans provides several options for the cluster membership provider, including Azure Table Storage, SQL Server, Apache ZooKeeper, Consul IO, and AWS DynamoDB. Membership is an extensibility point, with community-provided plug-ins for additional providers such as Redis, Kubernetes, MongoDB, and CosmosDB. For development and testing, an in-memory table can be used.

Summary

In this chapter, we explored what Grains and Silos are, digging a little into how they work and what guarantees they provide the application developer.

Grains are the unit of compute in an Orleans system and in the absence of failure offer several guarantees including at-most-once message delivery, single activation across the cluster, and turn-based concurrency.

Silos host the Grains, providing the message delivery and execution runtime. Silos cooperate and are members of a cluster that is coordinated with an external system.

References

Hewitt, Carl; Bishop, Peter; Steiger, Richard (1973). "A Universal Modular Actor Formalism for Artificial Intelligence." IJCAI.

CHAPTER 3

Hello World

In this chapter, we discuss and build the various projects needed for a simple "Hello, World" program in Orleans. While we could build a Hello World in a single C# file, it is important to understand how to separate concerns and improve maintainability by organizing Orleans code into separate projects.

Project Structure

A solution built with Orleans typically comprises several projects:

- **Grains classes**: At the heart of an Orleans solution are the classes that implement the grains logic. These classes are typically located together in a single project, but they can be split across multiple projects for larger solutions.

- **Grains interfaces**: The client and grains both need to agree on the interfaces that the grains support. The grains interfaces therefore need to be located in their own project which is shared by both the client code and the grains projects.

- **Silos host**: The Orleans Silos which activates the grains needs to be hosted by a project, which will be responsible for its configuration and life cycle.

- **Client**: Calls to Orleans are typically mediated via an API, which we call the client. This could be an ASP.NET Core project or similar. A client project acts as a gateway to the Orleans cluster.

- **Tests**: We should unit test our grains code and maintain a separate project for testing.

© Richard Astbury 2022
R. Astbury, *Microsoft Orleans for Developers*, https://doi.org/10.1007/978-1-4842-8167-3_3

Note   It's likely you'll have several more projects, for unit testing, running your code in a local/production deployment, etc., but these represent the core. It's also possible to run Orleans without a client or indeed to combine all code in a single project, but this chapter describes the typical use case.

Organizing classes in this fashion provides a clear separation between the code that runs in the Silos and the code that runs out of the Silos.

This prevents the developer from inadvertently calling grains directly, requiring calls to be made via the Orleans client instead.

Grains Types

The best place to start on an Orleans project is to model your problem in terms of grains. This can also be one of the hardest parts of the project as it isn't always obvious how the real world maps to grains state and methods.

In some scenarios, the design can be quite obvious. In an Internet of Things case, the grains would represent a device, such as a temperature sensor. Grains could also be used to represent a system which has multiple devices, such as a building or vehicle with multiple sensors.

In a gaming scenario, grains would represent players, as well as the games that they can join or leave.

Your case may not be so obvious, and it may take a few attempts to find the best fit.

Building the grains interfaces is therefore the point at which you think about the messages that grains will support and therefore their role in the system.

IRobot

During my early teens, I loved reading the Isaac Asimov robot stories. They discussed some of the practicalities and ethics of having robots in everyday life from a 1950s sci-fi perspective. I expect, like me, you are eagerly awaiting US Robotics and Mechanical Men to start selling units. However, in the meantime, there's nothing stopping us from building a high-scale, cloud-based infrastructure to command/control these robots, for when they eventually arrive.

In this book, we'll build a grains that represents a robot. We will send instructions to the grains, which will hold the instructions as a list. The robot will call the same grains to retrieve the next instruction to perform.

Creating Your First Grains Interface

Note   We're using Ubuntu 20.10, .NET 5.0.1, and Visual Studio Code for these code samples, but it shouldn't make any difference which operating system or IDE you use; just use whatever you are most comfortable with.

To get started, create a new folder for an "Orleans Book" application.

```
mkdir orleans-book
cd orleans-book
```

We'll then create a class library called "OrleansBook.GrainInterfaces" which will contain the interfaces for our grains.

```
dotnet new classlib --name OrleansBook.GrainInterfaces
```

We need to add the `Microsoft.Orleans.Core.Abstractions` NuGet package which contains the various classes and interfaces that grains and their interfaces depend upon.

Orleans uses code generation to automatically build the proxy code for clients to call grains. There are a couple of choices for how this is done, but the preferred approach is to use the `Microsoft.Orleans.CodeGenerator.MSBuild` NuGet package which was introduced in Orleans 2.1.0. This package uses Roslyn under the covers and has a faster build time than its predecessor. To install these NuGet packages, run the following commands:

```
cd OrleansBook.GrainInterfaces
dotnet add package Microsoft.Orleans.Core.Abstractions
dotnet add package Microsoft.Orleans.CodeGenerator.MSBuild
```

We can delete the Class1.cs file and create a new cs file for our interface:
OrleansBook.GrainInterfaces/IRobotGrain.cs

```
using System.Threading.Tasks;
using Orleans;

namespace OrleansBook.GrainInterfaces
{
  public interface IRobotGrain: IGrainWithStringKey
  {
    Task AddInstruction(string instruction);
    Task<string> GetNextInstruction();
    Task<int> GetInstructionCount();
  }
}
```

This interface will allow us to add instructions for the robot and allow the robot to retrieve the next instruction. We can also get a count of the number of instructions the robot currently has.

There are a few things to note about this interface. First, it inherits from IGrainWithStringKey. All grains interfaces must inherit from one of the provided Orleans "IGrainWithXXX" interfaces.

These interfaces provide different types of keys by which grains are referred.

Note   Unlike normal C# classes, Grains have a long-lived identity, much like database record has a primary key. This allows the grains to be referred to from anywhere in the cluster or from processes outside the cluster, at any time, whether the grains is activated or not.

Picking the correct interface, and therefore key, you want to use will depend on your domain. The choices are

- **IGrainWithIntegerKey**: A single integer (long)

- **IGrainWithGuidKey**: A single GUID

- **IGrainWithStringKey**: A single string

- **IGrainWithGuidCompoundKey**: A GUID and a string combined

- **IGrainWithIntegerCompoundKey**: An integer (long) and a string combined

You may be wondering why all of these combinations are presented, when a single string can be used to model all of these. The answer lies in the way Orleans has evolved to support additional types of key, with string being a later addition. For our code example, we've gone for a string key, but choose whichever is the best fit for your use case.

Note   The IGrainWithXXX interfaces do not specify any members to be implemented in the deriving class and act purely to indicate to Orleans that the deriving class is a grains.

The next thing to note about the interface is that there is a method which returns a Task<int>.

Methods represent the messages that the Grains supports. Because talking to a grains may involve the network and a delay while the message waits for the grains to complete any outstanding calls, grains methods must always be asynchronous, requiring a Task as a return type. This must be the case even if the method itself contains only synchronous code.

Creating Your First Grains Class

Next, we will create the project which will contain the grains implementations. We'll call this "OrleansBook.GrainClasses."

```
cd ..
dotnet new classlib --name OrleansBook.GrainClasses
```

As before, we need to add the Microsoft.Orleans.Core.Abstractions and Microsoft.Orleans.CodeGenerator.MSBuild NuGet packages.

```
cd OrleansBook.GrainClasses
dotnet add package Microsoft.Orleans.Core.Abstractions
dotnet add package Microsoft.Orleans.CodeGenerator.MSBuild
```

We also need to add a reference to our Grains interfaces:

```
dotnet add reference
../OrleansBook.GrainInterfaces/OrleansBook.GrainInterfaces.csproj
```

As before, remove the Class1.cs file, and create a class for our grains implementation:
OrleansBook.GrainClasses/RobotGrain.cs

```csharp
using System.Threading.Tasks;
using Orleans;
using OrleansBook.GrainInterfaces;

namespace OrleansBook.GrainClasses
{
  using System;
  using System.Collections.Generic;
  using System.Threading.Tasks;
  using Orleans;
  using OrleansBook.GrainInterfaces;

  namespace OrleansBook.GrainClasses
  {
    public class RobotGrain : Grain, IRobotGrain
    {
      private Queue<string> instructions = new Queue<string>();

      public Task AddInstruction(string instruction)
      {
        this.instructions.Enqueue(instruction);
        return Task.CompletedTask;
      }

      public Task<int> GetInstructionCount()
      {
        return Task.FromResult(this.instructions.Count);
      }

      public Task<string> GetNextInstruction()
      {
        if (this.instructions.Count == 0)
```

```
    {
      return Task.FromResult<string>(null);
    }
    var instruction = this.instructions.Dequeue();
    return Task.FromResult(instruction);
    }
  }
 }
}
```

There are a few things to note about this class. It implements the IRobotGrain interface as you would expect, but it also inherits Grain. This is an abstract class that grains are required to inherit. Grain provides base methods to hook into grains life cycle events, control grains activation, and retrieve services Orleans provides. We'll explore these later on in the book.

You will also notice that we use Task.FromResult to wrap the result as a completed task. Even though our code doesn't perform any asynchronous operations, we must still use a Task.

The code is not thread safe, for example, if the GetNextInstruction method is called in parallel, it may throw if the queue is emptied after the count is checked, and the Dequeue method is called. In a typical C# program, there are a few ways to make the code thread safe, including the use of the lock keyword or a ConcurrentQueue.

However, in a grains, this code is not necessary. The code inside grains is executed using "turn-based concurrency." This feature of Orleans ensures that multiple calls to a grains take turns, one after the other, and are not executed simultaneously. This means that grains code does not need to include any special consideration for concurrency, making it easier to write and reason about.

Note   Turn-based concurrency requires simultaneous calls to a grains to be queued. By default, calls to a grains time out after 30 seconds with an exception being thrown in the client. You should design your application to avoid too much contention on a single grains activation, i.e., a "hot" grains. There are ways to handle this, which we will study later in the book.

Creating Your First Host

Orleans is not an application you download and run, like a database; it's a library that you include in your application, similar to ASP.NET. Therefore, we need to write an application which will host an Orleans Silos. This will be an executable we can run from the console.

```
cd ..
dotnet new console --name OrleansBook.Host
```

We need to add the NuGet package which contains the runtime elements for hosting a silos:

```
cd OrleansBook.Host
dotnet add package Microsoft.Orleans.Server
```

We also need to add references to our Grains project, as the Silos will need to have access to the grains implementations in order to activate them (or create them as objects).

```
dotnet add reference ../OrleansBook.GrainClasses/OrleansBook.
GrainClasses.csproj
```

We can then update the Program.cs file to start the Silos.
OrleansBook.Host/Program.cs

```
using System;
using System.Threading.Tasks;
using Orleans;
using Orleans.Hosting;
using OrleansBook.GrainClasses;

namespace OrleansBook.Host
{
  class Program
  {
    static async Task Main()
    {
      var host = new HostBuilder()
        .UseOrleans(builder => {
```

```
    builder.ConfigureApplicationParts(parts => parts.AddApplication
    Part(typeof(RobotGrain).Assembly).WithReferences())
      .UseLocalhostClustering();
  })
  .Build();

await host.StartAsync();

Console.WriteLine("Press enter to stop the Silo...");
Console.ReadLine();

await host.StopAsync();
    }
  }
}
```

There is a lot involved with starting a Silos. Orleans supports lots of configuration and extension points, and starting the Silos is the point at which most of this is declared.

The HostBuilder class carries an extension method UseOrleans, which provides us with a builder for configuring the Silos. This is in line with the approach ASP.NET Core takes for configuring a web server.

The .ConfigureApplicationParts() method is used to register your grains with the silos. Orleans will scan an assembly, and its references, for grains classes. Orleans just needs to know which assembly, or project, you're using.

Orleans supports numerous ways of organizing the servers participating in the cluster. As a simple starting point, UseLocalhostClustering() will just use the local machine. We'll look at alternatives later on in the book.

The Build() method will then create the Silos host, which we can then StartAsync and StopAsync.

Note   When the host starts, the Silos will open two ports. Port 22222 is opened for communication between Silos. Port 40000 is opened for Clients to connect to a Silos. All communication to and between Silos is TCP/IP, although you can configure your own transport if you wish.

You can then run the Orleans silos from the command line:

```
dotnet run
```

If everything works correctly, you should see

```
Press enter to stop the Silo...
```

The silos is ready for a connection from a client. Let's write that code next.

Creating Your First Client

Hosting your Silos is a great start, but it won't do anything until a client connects and sends requests, which in turn will activate Grains.

Let's build a separate client application.

Note   While we could run the client in the same application as the silos, it will make the solution easier to understand if we keep the two separate.

```
cd ..
dotnet new console --name OrleansBook.Client
```

We need to add a NuGet package which contains the libraries required by a client.

```
cd OrleansBook.Client
dotnet add package Microsoft.Orleans.Client
dotnet add package Microsoft.Orleans.CodeGenerator.MSBuild
```

We also need to add a reference to the grains interface project, so the client knows what types of Grains are hosted in the Silos and the methods they support.

```
dotnet add reference ../OrleansBook.GrainInterfaces/OrleansBook.
GrainInterfaces.csproj
```

You can then update the `Program.cs` file to connect to the Silos.
OrleansBook.Client/Program.cs

```
using System;
using System.Threading.Tasks;
using Orleans;
```

```
using Orleans.Configuration;
using OrleansBook.GrainInterfaces;

namespace OrleansBook.Client
{
  class Program
  {
    static async Task Main()
    {
      var client = new ClientBuilder()
        .UseLocalhostClustering()
        .Build();

      using (client)
      {
        await client.Connect();

        while (true)
        {
          Console.WriteLine("Please enter a robot name...");
          var grainId = Console.ReadLine();
          var grain = client.GetGrain<IRobotGrain>(grainId);

          Console.WriteLine("Please enter an instruction...");
          var instruction = Console.ReadLine();
          await grain.AddInstruction(instruction);

          var count = await grain.GetInstructionCount();
          Console.WriteLine($"{grainId} has {count} instruction(s)");}");

        }
      }
    }
  }
}
```

The Client is built in a very similar way to the host. It's important that the configuration for networking and clustering matches that of the host, so the client is able to connect to the cluster correctly.

Once Connect() is called on the client, you can start to send message to the grains.

In this example, the user is prompted for an ID of a grains. The Client then provides a grains reference that derives from IRobotGrain which allows us to call methods, in this case AddInstruction() and GetInstructionCount(). When a method call is made, the request along with any parameters is serialized and sent over the network to the Silos. The Silos will then activate the grains, if it is not activated already, and call the corresponding method on the grains class. The response is then sent back over the network, and the Task is resolved.

We can try this out by running the program.

```
dotnet run
```

We should see the program prompt us for input, and we can make calls to our grains.

```
Please enter a robot name...
Robbie
Please enter an instruction...
Do the dishes
Robbie has 1 instruction(s)
Please enter a robot name...
Robbie
Please enter an instruction...
Put out the trash
Robbie has 2 instruction(s)
Please enter a robot name...
Daneel
Please enter an instruction...
Save the human race
Daneel has 1 instruction(s)
```

You can see that the instruction counter for each grains activation is incremented for every call. We see grains "Robbie" count from 1 to 2. When "Daneel" is activated, its instruction count starts from 1.

You can restart the client code, and you'll see the host will maintain the active grains in memory, and the counters will not reset.

Note   Orleans will remove these grains from memory (deactivate) on a regular cycle if it sees they are no longer receiving messages. We haven't configured any persistence for these grains, so when this happens, the grains will be lost, and a subsequent call will get a fresh activation. We'll address this later in the book.

Summary

In this chapter, we created four projects to provide a basic structure to our solution. It may seem a bit heavy-handed to create four projects with only a single class in each of them, but there are good reasons for splitting the client and server aspects into physically separate projects, sharing only interfaces for the grains.

We will continue to build on this infrastructure and add more classes as we progress through the chapters.

CHAPTER 4

Debugging an Orleans Application

Our robot application is a pretty simple example so far, but before it gets any more complicated, it would be useful to get debugging information out of the system to help us diagnose any faults we encounter. In these scenarios, we need a methodology to debug Orleans projects. This chapter will cover some basics for how to get more information out of Orleans to help us diagnose these faults.

Logging

We can attach the debugger to the Silos Host or Client applications and add breakpoints to get an insight into what our grains are doing while the application is running. However, once the system is deployed, we have to rely on logging to get the information we need for diagnosing faults.

The `Microsoft.Extensions.Logging.Abstractions` NuGet package contains some generalized constructs for logging in .NET applications. We can take advantage of this abstractions, not just for our own logging, but for consuming the log information from Orleans itself.

In the Host project, we will add a reference to the `Microsoft.Extensions.Logging.Console` NuGet package, so we can start logging data to the console.

```
cd OrleansBook.Host
dotnet add package Microsoft.Extensions.Logging.Console
```

If you add a reference to the logging namespace:

```
using Microsoft.Extensions.Logging;
```

© Richard Astbury 2022
R. Astbury, *Microsoft Orleans for Developers*, https://doi.org/10.1007/978-1-4842-8167-3_4

You can configure logging in the Silos HostBuilder:

```
builder.ConfigureLogging(x => x.AddConsole())
```

Putting the whole thing together now looks like this:

OrleansBook.Host/Program.cs

```
using System;
using System.Threading.Tasks;
using Microsoft.Extensions.Logging;
using Orleans;
using Orleans.Hosting;
using OrleansBook.GrainClasses;

namespace OrleansBook.Host
{
  class Program
  {
    static async Task Main()
    {
      var host = new HostBuilder()
        .UseOrleans(builder => {
          builder.ConfigureApplicationParts(parts => parts.AddApplication
          Part(typeof(RobotGrain).Assembly).WithReferences())
          .UseLocalhostClustering()
          .ConfigureLogging(logging => logging.AddConsole())
        })
        .Build();

      await host.StartAsync();

      Console.WriteLine("Press enter to stop the Silo...");
      Console.ReadLine();

      await host.StopAsync();
    }
  }
}
```

When you run the Host, you'll now see much more output on the Console. In fact, you'll probably see much more than you want. You can raise the minimum log level to whatever is the most appropriate.

```
logging.SetMinimumLevel(LogLevel.Warning);
```

If you start with Warnings, you can then lower the level if your application is not working as expected, and allow more telemetry through until you diagnose the fault.

The Client project can be given exactly the same treatment.

```
cd OrleansBook.Client
dotnet add package Microsoft.Extensions.Logging.Console
```

OrleansBook.Client/Program.cs

```
using System;
using System.Threading.Tasks;
using Orleans;
using Orleans.Configuration;
using Microsoft.Extensions.Logging;
using OrleansBook.GrainInterfaces;

namespace OrleansBook.Client
{
  class Program
  {
    static async Task Main(string[] args)
    {
      var client = new ClientBuilder()
        .UseLocalhostClustering()
        .ConfigureLogging(logging =>
        {
          logging.AddConsole();
          logging.SetMinimumLevel(LogLevel.Warning);
        })
        .Build();

      using (client)
      {
```

```
      await client.Connect();

      while (true)
      {
        Console.WriteLine("Please enter a robot name...");
        var grainId = Console.ReadLine();
        var grain = client.GetGrain<IRobotGrain>(grainId);

        Console.WriteLine("Please enter an instruction...");
        var instruction = Console.ReadLine();
        await grain.AddInstruction(instruction);

        var count = await grain.GetInstructionCount();
        Console.WriteLine($"{grainId} has {count}
instruction(s)");          }
      }
    }
  }
}
```

To write logging information from within grains, we need to add the logging abstractions NuGet package to the GrainClasses project:

```
cd OrleansBook.GrainClasses
dotnet add package Microsoft.Extensions.Logging.Abstractions
```

We can then add an ILogger<RobotGrain> parameter to the grain's constructor and start writing log information to it.

```
using System.Threading.Tasks;
using Microsoft.Extensions.Logging;
using Orleans;
using OrleansBook.GrainInterfaces;

namespace OrleansBook.GrainClasses
{
  public class RobotGrain : Grain, IRobotGrain
  {
    ILogger<RobotGrain> logger;
```

```
public RobotGrain(ILogger<RobotGrain> logger)
{
  this.logger = logger;
}

private Queue<string> instructions = new Queue<string>();

public Task AddInstruction(string instruction)
{
  var key = this.GetPrimaryKeyString();
  this.logger.LogWarning("{Key} adding '{Instruction}'",
    key, instruction);
  this.instructions.Enqueue(instruction);
  return Task.CompletedTask;
}

public Task<int> GetInstructionCount()
{
  return Task.FromResult(this.instructions.Count);
}

public Task<string> GetNextInstruction()
{
  if (this.instructions.Count == 0)
  {
    return Task.FromResult<string>(null);
  }
  var instruction = this.instructions.Dequeue();
  var key = this.GetPrimaryKeyString();
  this.logger.LogWarning("{Key} adding '{Instruction}'",
    key, instruction);
  return Task.FromResult(instruction);
  }
 }
}
```

Note   In the line that writes the log information, we get the identity of the grains using `GetPrimaryKeyString()`; this is a method provided by Orleans to get the ID of the grains. This is the same string the client code uses when getting a reference to the grains. This is often useful, not only for the purposes of logging, but more generally as grains code often uses the identity of the grains when loading data from external systems, for example.

We have logged a warning in this example, just to make sure we can see the logging on the console output. Such a message would normally be regarded as "Information" or "Trace."

The grains class receives the logger as a parameter on the grains constructor, without us having to configure anything. Orleans supports dependency injection in the same way controllers in ASP.NET do. The logger is one of the classes injected by default; we can of course add our own.

Metrics

Orleans also emits a number of metrics that can be consumed to understand the runtime performance of a system. This can give you a great insight when tracking down performance problems.

Configuring Application Insights

The easiest way to consume these metrics is to use Azure Application Insights. The `Microsoft.Orleans.OrleansTelemetryConsumers.AI` NuGet package provides the necessary telemetry consumers and publishes this data to Application Insights for you in both the Client and the Host:

Host configuration:

```
builder
 .AddApplicationInsightsTelemetryConsumer("INSTRUMENTATION_KEY");
```

Client configuration:

```
new ClientBuilder()
 .AddApplicationInsightsTelemetryConsumer("INSTRUMENTATION_KEY");
```

There are similar NuGet packages for New Relic, Windows Performance Counters, and community-contributed package for Elastic Search.

Writing a Custom Consumer

If you wish to capture telemetry and store it elsewhere, you can write your own consumer.

You will need to write a class that implements IMetricTelemetryConsumer and then register it:

```
builder
  .Configure<TelemetryOptions>(options =>
    options.AddConsumer<MyCustomConsumer>())
```

I won't go into the detail of implementing this class, but knowing this extensibility point is here means that it's an option if needed.

There are over 120 different counters reported by Orleans. They cover everything from average request latency to the size of the serialization buffer pool. If you're diagnosing a performance issue, there might be a metric there which proves to be useful.

Summary

Logging to the console is a great way to see trace information while developing, but on a production system, we should be looking for a logging destination that can store our logs and allow us to search/filter the data.

There are numerous Microsoft and third-party NuGet packages to allow us to forward log and telemetry data to third-party destinations, such as Azure Application Insights, New Relic, and Elmah.

For more information on logging in .NET, see this page: `https://docs.microsoft.com/en-us/aspnet/core/fundamentals/logging/`.

For performance issues, the telemetry from Orleans can be captured and forwarded to third parties or handled by our own custom consumer.

In the next chapter, we'll see another option for logging and instrumentation – the Orleans Dashboard.

CHAPTER 5

Orleans Dashboard

The Orleans Dashboard is a community-contributed project which adds a real-time dashboard to Orleans, allowing you to get a visual insight into the performance of your application.

The Dashboard is particularly useful during the development of a project, as it can give you a quick insight into the behavior of the system.

Installation

The dashboard project is located in the OrleansContrib organization in GitHub (https://github.com/OrleansContrib/OrleansDashboard).

You can install it in the Host project by adding the OrleansDashboard NuGet package.

```
cd OrleansBook.Host
dotnet add package OrleansDashboard
```

You can then add it using the host configuration:

```
var host = new HostBuilder()
  .UseOrleans(builder => {
    builder.UseDashboard();
  })
  .Build();
```

Now when you start the host, the dashboard is also started, which opens up a web server on port 8080. You can connect a web browser to this port to view the dashboard. If your silos is running locally, use http://localhost:8080.

© Richard Astbury 2022
R. Astbury, *Microsoft Orleans for Developers*, https://doi.org/10.1007/978-1-4842-8167-3_5

Note The Dashboard must be configured for every host in the cluster. You can connect your web browser to any of the hosts to see the dashboard, and you will get the same view, with the exception of the streaming log data which is host specific.

You should expect to see something like the screenshot in Figure 5-1.

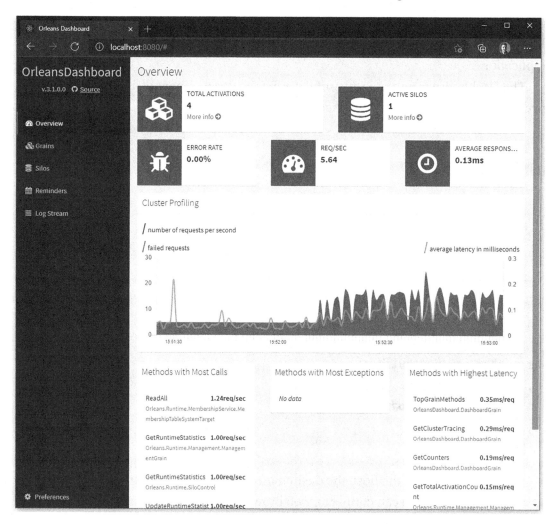

Figure 5-1. *Orleans Dashboard Homepage*

The main dashboard shows a summary at the top of the total number of activations (i.e., the total number of active grains in the whole cluster) and the number of Silos participating in the cluster. The Dashboard intercepts every grains call and is able to build a picture of the total number of grains calls per second, the number of those that threw exceptions, and the average response times.

These statistics are displayed as headline figures at the top of the page and again as a graph showing how they have trended over the last few minutes.

Summaries are then shown of the grains methods with the most calls, the most exceptions, and the highest latency.

This is a great way to quickly understand the health of your system and to spot areas that might be running slowly or throwing errors.

The dashboard allows you to drill down into the data, either by looking at the Silos or the Grains.

Grains Type Overview

Drilling into a grains type provides an overview of how that type is performing across the Orleans cluster.

The total number of activations of this grains type are shown, along with the error rate, requests per second, and average latency. See Figure 5-2.

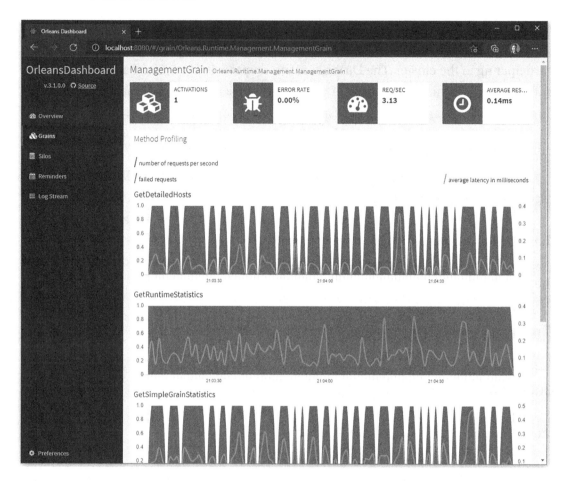

Figure 5-2. *Orleans Dashboard Grains Type Details*

Each method of the grains type is then shown as a separate graph, showing the number of requests, failed requests, and latency. This profiling allows you to understand the individual behavior of each of the methods on your grains, making it easy to spot underperforming areas of the system.

Note   The Dashboard, and Orleans itself, internally uses Grains which are shown in the Dashboard. They are marked as either "System" or "Dashboard" Grains and can be hidden from view in the preferences menu.

Silos Overview

As shown in Figure 5-3, the Silos overview shows the resources the Silos is consuming (CPU and memory) and the grains usage. This is a metric Orleans generates which indicates the percentage of active grains that have recently been used. You could expect unused grains to be deactivated in Orleans' next deactivation cycle.

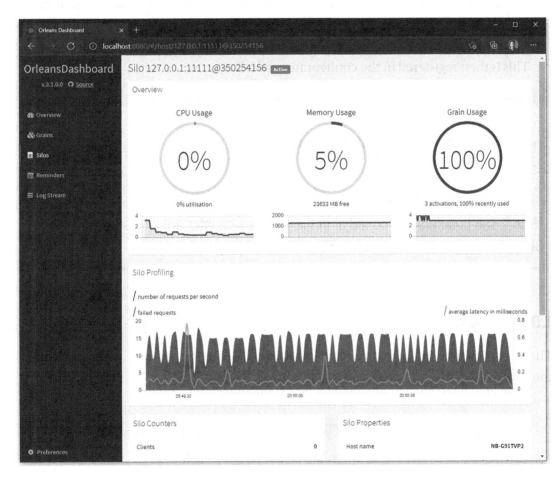

Figure 5-3. *Orleans Dashboard Silos Details*

By default, the CPU and Memory metrics are not shown. An additional NuGet package is required which is dependent on your operating system.

For Linux, use `Microsoft.Orleans.OrleansTelemetryConsumers.Linux`.

```
dotnet add package Microsoft.Orleans.OrleansTelemetryConsumers.Linux
```

41

This is then registered in the configuration as follows:

```
builder
  .UseDashboard()
  .UseLinuxEnvironmentStatistics()
  .Build();
```

Or on Windows, use Microsoft.Orleans.OrleansTelemetryConsumers.Counters.

```
dotnet add package Microsoft.Orleans.OrleansTelemetryConsumers.Counters
```

This is then registered in the configuration as follows:

```
builder
  .UseDashboard()
  .UsePerfCounterEnvironmentStatistics()
  .Build();
```

Note   The counters we looked at in the previous chapter are also shown for each Silos, if you click the "view all" link on the counters panel.

Log Stream

The trace data from an individual Silos can be streamed to the browser accessible from the "Log Stream" menu. See Figure 5-4.

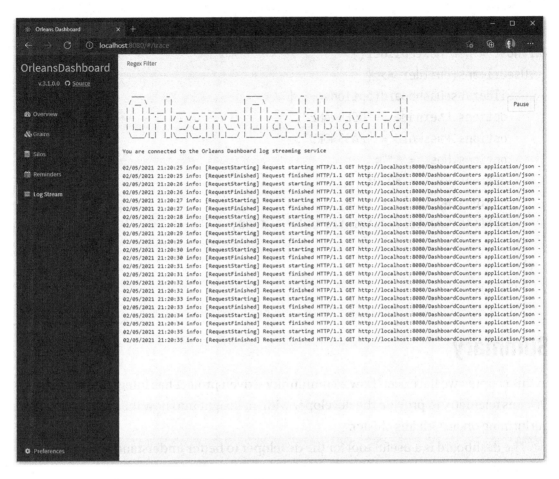

Figure 5-4. *Orleans Dashboard Log Trace*

The log stream can move very rapidly, so a pause button allows you to stop the view from being updated. You can also filter lines with a regex.

Advanced Usage

The dashboard supports some configuration options:

- Basic Authentication username and password.

- The host name and port number the web server uses.

- The reporting interval, defaulted to 1 second.

- The dashboard can be added as an ASP.NET middleware component rather than self-hosting its own web server.

These options are configured when adding the dashboard in the SiloHostBuilder:

```
var host = new HostBuilder()
  .UseOrleans(builder => {
    builder.UseDashboard(options => {
      options.Username = "USERNAME";
      options.Password = "PASSWORD";
      options.Host = "*";
      options.Port = 8080;
      options.HostSelf = true;
      options.CounterUpdateIntervalMs = 1000;
    })
  })
  .Build();
```

Summary

In this chapter, we have seen how a community-driven project has integrated with the Orleans telemetry to provide the developer with an insight into how their application is performing on an Orleans cluster.

The dashboard is a useful tool for the developer to better understand what's happening inside their Orleans system.

CHAPTER 6

Adding Persistence

In this chapter, we will build upon the project structure we set out in Chapter 5 and add durable state, or persistence, as a feature to our grains.

Orleans has an in-built persistence feature. However, Orleans does not store data within the cluster; instead, data is stored in an external storage system of your choice. Orleans provides the plumbing for the grain's state to be serialized and stored and to automatically load this state when a grains is reactivated.

This is an entirely optional feature. If you wish to load and save data yourself, you can. For example, you may have existing data access classes for writing data to a SQL Server, which as long as it's async, you can use from your grains.

Robot State

We will start by creating a POCO class which will hold the state we wish to persist. In this case, we will store the instructions that the robot will carry out. Our grains will store these instructions so that the robot can retrieve the next task it is to perform.

Add the following class to the OrleansBook.GrainClasses project:

OrleansBook.GrainClasses/RobotState.cs

```
namespace OrleansBook.GrainClasses
{
  public class RobotState
  {
    public Queue<string> Instructions { get; set; }
      = new Queue<string>();
  }
}
```

© Richard Astbury 2022
R. Astbury, *Microsoft Orleans for Developers*, https://doi.org/10.1007/978-1-4842-8167-3_6

Note   The state is added to the grains classes project. The internal state of the grains is no concern to the grains client and is not part of the grains interface.

Adding State to the Grains

The concerns of reading and writing state are provided by the IPersistentState<TState> service. This is passed into the grain's constructor, and the grains should hold a reference to this object as a private member variable.

The grains can have multiple state objects, each with a different backing store if required. You just need to provide more IPersistentState<TState> arguments on the Grain's constructor.

The actual code to read and write the data is decoupled from the grains. A pluggable storage provider is used. In the grains, we just need to provide the name of the store we want to use, which should match a provider registered in the host configuration.

A [PersistentState] attribute is used in the arguments on the grains constructor to indicate the provider to use.

```
public Grain(
  [PersistentState("stateName", "storeName")]
  IPersistentState<TState> state)
{ ... }
```

We will see how storage providers are registered later in this chapter.

The persistent state service provides methods to save, load, and clear the stored state. It also provides an optional ETag property used for optimistic locking of the underlying data.

This stops data from being overwritten in the case that it has changed since the record was last fetched. This can arise if two clients attempt to write to the same record at the same time. Instead of last-write-wins, which could result in data being lost, the second write will get an error, and the client will have to reload and retry.

The storage provider refreshes the value of the ETag with each revision of the state. The storage provider can then use the ETag to see if the stored state has changed since the last revision. If ETags do no match, it will reject the write, throwing an exception.

This is not something you would normally expect to happen, but it is possible when the system is undergoing a network partition. In this case, multiple activations of the same grains may temporarily appear, as Orleans prefers availability over consistency, which could result in unexpected writes to storage. The ETag ensures that the underlying state remains strongly consistent even under these scenarios.

Not all storage providers implement ETags, in which case the value will always be null.

Let's go ahead and add the RobotState to the RobotGrain!

OrleansBook.GrainClasses.RobotGrain.cs

```
using System;
using System.Collections.Generic;
using System.Threading.Tasks;
using Microsoft.Extensions.Logging;
using Orleans;
using Orleans.Runtime;
using OrleansBook.GrainInterfaces;

namespace OrleansBook.GrainClasses
{
  public class RobotGrain : Grain, IRobotGrain
  {
    ILogger<RobotGrain> logger;
    IPersistentState<RobotState> state;

    public RobotGrain(
      ILogger<RobotGrain> logger,
      [PersistentState("robotState", "robotStateStore")]
      IPersistentState<RobotState> state)
    {
      this.logger = logger;
      this.state = state;
    }

    public async Task AddInstruction(string instruction)
    {
      var key = this.GetPrimaryKeyString();
      this.logger.LogWarning($"{key} adding '{instruction}'");
```

```
    this.state.State.Instructions.Enqueue(instruction);
    await this.state.WriteStateAsync();
  }

  public Task<int> GetInstructionCount()
  {
    return Task.FromResult(
      this.state.State.Instructions.Count);
  }

  public async Task<string> GetNextInstruction()
  {
    if (this.state.State.Instructions.Count == 0)
    {
      return null;
    }

    var instruction = this.state.State.Instructions.Dequeue();
    var key = this.GetPrimaryKeyString();

    this.logger.LogWarning(
      $"{key} returning '{instruction}'");

    await this.state.WriteStateAsync();
    return instruction;
  }
 }
}
```

You'll notice that when the state is changed, either by an instruction being added or removed, the state is persisted by calling WriteStateAsync(). Reading the number of instructions in the queue doesn't require the state to change and can be answered directly with the in-memory state. This is where Orleans provides a performance benefit. The more calls that can be answered using data that's in memory, the less the calls to the storage tier and the faster the response times.

State is automatically loaded for us when the grains activates, so there is no need in this example to call ReadStateAsync().

Configuring the Storage Provider

The OrleansBook.Host project will need to be modified to register a Storage Provider, which will respond to the grains' requests to read, write, or clear state, and talk to the underlying storage system.

Orleans has a number of out-of-the-box providers. The NuGet packages for the various providers are

- **Microsoft.Orleans.Persistence.AdoNet** for databases supported by ADO.NET

- **Microsoft.Orleans.Persistence.AzureStorage** for Azure Blog Storage, Azure Table Storage, and CosmosDB

- **Microsoft.Orleans.Persistence.DynamoDB** for Amazon DynamoDB

There are providers for additional storage systems in the OrleansContrib organization on GitHub (https://github.com/OrleansContrib).

An in-memory provider is supplied for local development, which is what we will use for now. This can be added by adding .AddMemoryGrainStorageAsDefault() to the SiloHostBuilder. Your host should now look like this:

OrleansBook.Host/Program.cs

```
using System;
using System.Threading.Tasks;
using Microsoft.Extensions.Logging;
using Orleans;
using Orleans.Hosting;
using Orleans.Statistics;
using OrleansBook.GrainClasses;

namespace OrleansBook.Host
{
  class Program
  {
    static async Task Main()
    {
      var host = new SiloHostBuilder()
```

```
        .ConfigureApplicationParts(parts => parts.AddApplicationPart(typeof
        (RobotGrain).Assembly).WithReferences())
        .UseLocalhostClustering()
        .ConfigureLogging(logging =>
        {
          logging.AddConsole();
          logging.SetMinimumLevel(LogLevel.Information);
        })
        .UseDashboard()
        .UseLinuxEnvironmentStatistics()
        .AddMemoryGrainStorage("robotStateStore")
        .Build();

    await host.StartAsync();

    Console.WriteLine("Press enter to stop the Silo...");
    Console.ReadLine();

    await host.StopAsync();
    }
  }
}
```

Note   Using the Orleans Storage Provider model is totally optional. If you wish to load and save state from an alternative data store, you can simply connect to it from any asynchronous API. By overriding the OnActivateAsync() method, the grains can load state such that it's ready whenever the grains is activated. The in-built persistence can save a significant amount of development time, as no further data access code is required.

You should be careful when updating the grains state class. If the grains state is updated in a new version of your software, if the storage provider is unable to deserialize the state persisted by your previous version, you may find that grains cannot be activated.

One strategy is to use a version-tolerant serializer, such as JSON.

Summary

In this sample, we saw how a storage provider can take care of the data access concerns of a grains and make a durable state property that can be loaded and saved to a choice of backing stores.

This is a convenient feature, allowing developers to focus on the business logic in the grains, rather than data access code.

However, caution should be used when considering updates to the grains state class. We must ensure the storage provider and state are always backward compatible.

CHAPTER 7

Adding ASP.NET Core

So far, our solution uses a simple console application as the client. A more realistic scenario is for Orleans to be fronted by a Web API, such as ASP.NET Core.

Orleans should never be exposed directly to the Internet. Its interface is intended only for use on an internal network as it doesn't deal with the authentication and authorization concerns required with public-facing services.

It's not necessary to build a Web API for Orleans; it's equally valid to use it in a completely headless deployment, such as processing messages from a queue.

Adding an ASP.NET Web API Project

Let's create a new ASP.NET Core web application and connect it to Orleans. We can do this from the command line:

```
dotnet new webapi --name OrleansBook.WebApi
```

As we did before with the OrleansBook.GrainClient project, we need to add references to NuGet packages and the OrleansBook.GrainInterfaces project.

```
cd OrleansBook.WebApi
dotnet add package Microsoft.Orleans.Core.Abstractions
dotnet add package Microsoft.Orleans.CodeGenerator.MSBuild
dotnet add reference ../OrleansBook.GrainInterfaces/OrleansBook.
GrainInterfaces.csproj
```

The API will act as a client for Orleans, converting HTTP requests into grains calls and back again. Therefore, we need to add the Orleans Client initialization code as we did for the OrleansBook.GrainClient project. This is placed in the Startup.cs file, alongside the ASP.NET configuration.

© Richard Astbury 2022
R. Astbury, *Microsoft Orleans for Developers*, https://doi.org/10.1007/978-1-4842-8167-3_7

OrleansBook.WebApi/Startup.cs

```csharp
using System;
using System.Threading.Tasks;
using Microsoft.AspNetCore.Builder;
using Microsoft.AspNetCore.Hosting;
using Microsoft.Extensions.Configuration;
using Microsoft.Extensions.DependencyInjection;
using Microsoft.Extensions.Hosting;
using Orleans;

namespace OrleansBook.WebApi
{
  public class Startup
  {
    public Startup(IConfiguration configuration)
    {
      Configuration = configuration;
    }

    public IConfiguration Configuration { get; }

    async Task<IClusterClient> ConnectToOrleans()
    {
      var client = new ClientBuilder()
        .UseLocalhostClustering()
        .Build();

      await client.Connect();
      return client;
    }

    public void ConfigureServices(IServiceCollection services)
    {
      var client = ConnectToOrleans().Result;
      services.AddSingleton<IClusterClient>(client);

      services.AddControllers();
    }
```

```
public void Configure(IApplicationBuilder app, IWebHostEnvironment env)
{
  if (env.IsDevelopment())
  {
    app.UseDeveloperExceptionPage();
  }

  app.UseRouting();

  app.UseEndpoints(endpoints =>
  {
    endpoints.MapControllers();
  });
}
}
}
```

Once Open() is called on IClusterClient, the connection to the cluster is open and ready to use. We add a reference to it as a singleton service in ASP.NET. This then makes it available to controllers. A singleton ensures that a single instance of the client is maintained and kept open for every call, as there is an overhead in opening the client connection. The client is thread safe, so there is no problem with multiple controller instances calling it simultaneously.

Calling Grains from Controller Actions

Next, we'll create a controller which will call the IRobotGrain grains. The controller will expose GET/POST actions which will retrieve/create the instructions respectively by calling the appropriate methods of the grains.

By providing an IClusterClient parameter on the controller's constructor, we can create a reference to the grains using an ID provided on the URL (i.e., http://localhost:5000/robot/ROBOT_123/instruction).

OrleansBook/RobotController.cs

```
using System;
using Orleans;
using System.Threading.Tasks;
```

```
using Microsoft.AspNetCore.Mvc;
using OrleansBook.GrainInterfaces;

namespace OrleansBook.WebApi.Controllers
{
  [ApiController]
  public class RobotController : ControllerBase
  {
    private readonly IClusterClient _client;

    public RobotController(IClusterClient client)
    {
      _client = client;
    }

    [HttpGet]
    [Route("robot/{name}/instruction")]
    public Task<string> Get(string name)
    {
      var grain = this._client.GetGrain<IRobotGrain>(name);
      return grain.GetNextInstruction();
    }

    [HttpPost]
    [Route("robot/{name}/instruction")]
    public async Task<IActionResult> Post(string name, StorageValue value)
    {
      var grain = this._client.GetGrain<IRobotGrain>(name);
      await grain.AddInstruction(value.Value);
      return Ok();
    }

  }
}
```

You can now start the web app (and the OrleansBook.Host project)

```
dotnet run
```

To test the API, we can use cURL to create requests (or you can use any tool you are familiar with that can generate HTTP POST and GET requests).

To set a value, we can POST some JSON:

```
curl \
  --header "Content-Type: application/json" \
  --request POST \
  --data '{"Value": "Clean the house"}' \
  http://localhost:5000/robot/robbie/instruction
```

We can then read that value with a GET:

```
curl http://localhost:5000/robot/robbie/instruction
```

This returns:

```
Clean the house
```

Our example here doesn't deal with any of authentication or authorization concerns, but these aspects wouldn't differ from any conventional web application in ASP. NET Core.

Summary

In this chapter, we added ASP.NET as a front end to Orleans to provide a Web API for our robot controlling system.

We saw how controllers can be passed the `IClusterClient` as a singleton service, allowing actions to make calls to grains in response to HTTP requests.

CHAPTER 8

Unit Testing

Some of the first code you'll want to write is a test, to make sure the logic in your Grains is correct.

As we have discussed in this book, Grains are hosted by Silos, which provide turn-based concurrency, so to correctly test a grains, we need to use a Silos or a cluster of Silos.

Orleans makes this easy for us by providing a Test Cluster, which carries the same semantics as a real Silos, but without such a configuration burden.

In this chapter, we will write a unit test which will use the Test Cluster to send messages to our grains in a new test project.

Adding a Test Project

We'll start by creating a new project to host our tests:

```
dotnet new mstest -name OrleansBook.Tests
```

We'll then add the required NuGet packages:

```
cd OrleansBook.Tests
dotnet add package Microsoft.Orleans.TestingHost
dotnet add package moq
dotnet add reference ..\OrleansBook.GrainInterfaces\
dotnet add reference ..\OrleansBook.GrainClasses\
```

Let's just examine what these commands do. First, we add the `Microsoft.Orleans.TestingHost` package, which contains everything we need to run the test host. The next NuGet package is the moq, which is a library which allows us to create mocks of interfaces. We'll see this in action later in the chapter. We then add references to the existing Grains Interfaces and Grains Classes projects, which will be our test subjects.

© Richard Astbury 2022
R. Astbury, *Microsoft Orleans for Developers*, https://doi.org/10.1007/978-1-4842-8167-3_8

Next, remove the UnitTest1.cs example test, and create a new file called
RobotGrainTests.cs.

We'll start by creating the basic boiler plate code for testing grains.

```csharp
using System.Threading.Tasks;
using Microsoft.VisualStudio.TestTools.UnitTesting;
using Orleans.TestingHost;
using OrleansBook.GrainInterfaces;

namespace OrleansBook.Tests
{
  [TestClass]
  public class RobotGrainTests
  {
    static TestCluster cluster;

    [ClassInitialize]
    public static void ClassInit(TestContext context)
    {
      cluster = new TestClusterBuilder()
        .Build();

      cluster.Deploy();
    }

    [ClassCleanup]
    public static void ClassCleanup()
    {
      cluster.StopAllSilos();
    }

    [TestMethod]
    public async Task TestInstructions()
    {
      var robot = cluster.GrainFactory
        .GetGrain<IRobotGrain>("test");
```

```
    // add code to test the grain
  }
 }
}
```

The ClassInit and ClassCleanup methods are run before and after the test
methods, respectively. They initialize and dispose of the test silos and maintain a private
static member variable "cluster," which holds a reference to this silos. The test methods
can then make use of cluster to get a reference to the grains factory, to make calls
to grains.

The test cluster will have the same runtime semantics as a real silos, providing a more
accurate test environment than simply calling grains methods directly from a unit test.

The preceding code will allow you to test a simple grains, but our grains requires a
little more configuration to allow us to test the storage provider.

Adding Silos Configuration

The TestHostBuilder has a AddSiloBuilderConfigurator<T>() method which allows
you to register a class that implements ISiloConfigurator, which can be used to
provide additional configuration for the silos.

We need to provide an implementation of ISiloConfiguration which will register
a storage provider for our state. We can use a mock instead of writing a concrete
implementation of the storage provider; we just configure our mock so the State
property returns an instance of RobotState, as the grains expects.

The mock storage provider is then registered as a service, allowing the grains to
receive the object on its constructor.

```
class SiloBuilderConfigurator : ISiloConfigurator
{
  public void Configure(ISiloBuilder hostBuilder)
  {
    hostBuilder.AddMemoryGrainStorage("robotStateStore");

    var mockState = new Mock<IPersistentState<RobotState>>();
    mockState.SetupGet(s => s.State).Returns(new RobotState());

    hostBuilder.ConfigureServices(services =>
```

```
  {
    Services
      .AddSingleton<IPersistentState<RobotState>>(
        mockState.Object);
    services.AddSingleton<ILogger<RobotGrain>>(
        new Mock<ILogger<RobotGrain>>().Object);
  });
  }
}
```

To register this configuration with the TestCluster, we call the AddSiloBuilderConfiguration method using our configuration class as the generic "T" argument.

```
[ClassInitialize]
public static void ClassInit(TestContext context)
{
  cluster = new TestClusterBuilder()
    .AddSiloBuilderConfigurator<SiloBuilderConfigurator>()
    .Build();
  cluster.Deploy();
}
```

Adding a Test Method

We can now add some lines of code to our test method to check the grains functions as expected:

```
[TestMethod]
public async Task TestInstructions()
{
  var robot = cluster.GrainFactory.GetGrain<IRobotGrain>("test");

  await robot.AddInstruction("Do the dishes");
  await robot.AddInstruction("Take out the trash");
  await robot.AddInstruction("Do the laundry");
```

```
Assert.AreEqual(3, await robot.GetInstructionCount());
Assert.AreEqual(
  await robot.GetNextInstruction(), "Do the dishes");
Assert.AreEqual(
  await robot.GetNextInstruction(), "Take out the trash");
Assert.AreEqual(
  await robot.GetNextInstruction(), "Do the laundry");
Assert.IsNull(await robot.GetNextInstruction());
Assert.AreEqual(0, await robot.GetInstructionCount());
}
```

The test code adds some instructions for the robot to undertake. We then call GetNextInstruction to ensure we get the instructions in the correct order.

To run the tests, type

```
dotnet test
```

Summary

In this chapter, we've seen how we can use the TestClusterBuilder to build a test cluster which we can use to unit test our grains. We have seen how we can customize the configuration of the test cluster to include the services that our grains needs. We used moq, a common mocking library to simulate one of our storage dependencies which we registered for the grains to consume.

Unit testing is a critical part of software development, and being able to test our grains logic in isolation is a useful way of verifying that the code we write is correct.

CHAPTER 9

Streams

Publish-Subscribe is a useful pattern for decoupling code both in terms of separation of concerns and temporal coupling. Pub-Sub is a pattern and is used extensively in distributed systems and microservice architectures. Orleans natively supports Pub-Sub implemented as Orleans Streams.

Like the Actors, Streams in Orleans are virtual. This means they do not need to be explicitly created or disposed, and can be used at any time. They also work symmetrically inside a silos using a grains or outside a silos as an Orleans Client.

In this chapter, we will add a stream to robot application which will publish a feed of instructions as they are executed. This would allow you to keep up to date with what your robot is up to. The Web API will subscribe to the changes and write them to console, but in a more complete system, you could use WebSocket or notifications to push this information to the user.

Stream Providers

Out of the box Orleans has a memory-based stream provider (Simple Messaging Stream), where messages are not durable and are subject to the unreliability of the network. Messages are also delivered immediately with no buffer.

Similar to the storage system, Orleans Streams support different underlying providers to allow streams to be durable. This allows you to work to one common API without taking a hard dependency on any particular provider, and offer different guarantees and semantics, depending on which provider is selected.

Additional stream providers are available via NuGet:

- **Microsoft.Orleans.OrleansServiceBus** for Azure Service Bus and Event Hubs

- **Microsoft.Orleans.Streaming.AzureStorage** for Azure Storage Queues

65

© Richard Astbury 2022
R. Astbury, *Microsoft Orleans for Developers*, https://doi.org/10.1007/978-1-4842-8167-3_9

- **Microsoft.Orleans.Streaming.SQS** for AWS Simple Queuing Service

- **Microsoft.Orleans.OrleansGCPUtils** for Google Cloud Platform PubSub service

Alternatively, you can write your own adaptor to the provider of your choice.

Configuring the Host

To configure streaming, we add the provider we wish to use in the `SiloHostBuilder`. In this case, we will use the Simple Message Stream, which is included with Orleans. This stream provider requires a storage provider which by default is called "`PubSubStore`." This is just used to persist the queue names rather than the messages themselves. We therefore also add a storage provider of that name, using the built-in (nondurable) memory-based storage.

OrleansBook.Host/Program.cs

```
using System;
using System.Threading.Tasks;
using Microsoft.Extensions.Logging;
using Orleans;
using Orleans.Hosting;
using Orleans.Statistics;
using OrleansBook.GrainClasses;

namespace OrleansBook.Host
{
  class Program
  {
    static async Task Main()
    {
      var host = new HostBuilder()
        .UseOrleans(builder => {
          builder.ConfigureApplicationParts(parts => parts.AddApplication
          Part(typeof(RobotGrain).Assembly).WithReferences())
            .UseLocalhostClustering()
            .ConfigureLogging(logging =>
```

```
      {
        logging.AddConsole();
        logging.SetMinimumLevel(LogLevel.Information);
      })
      .UseDashboard()
      .UseLinuxEnvironmentStatistics()
      .AddMemoryGrainStorageAsDefault()
      .AddMemoryGrainStorage("PubSubStore")
      .AddSimpleMessageStreamProvider("SMSProvider");
    })
    .Build();

  await host.StartAsync();

  Console.WriteLine("Press enter to stop the Silo...");
  Console.ReadLine();

  await host.StopAsync();
    }
  }
}
```

The host is now ready to support streaming.

Publishing Events from Grains

To publish information about the tasks our robot is undertaking, we'll need a new class
to represent the message. This will have properties for the name of the robot and the
description of the task. As this class will be used by both the client code and server code,
it's a natural fit for the "GrainInterfaces" project.

OrleansBook.GrainInterfaces/InstructionMessage.cs

```
namespace OrleansBook.GrainInterfaces
{
  public class InstructionMessage
  {
    public InstructionMessage()
    { }
```

```
    public InstructionMessage(string instruction, string robot)
    {
      this.Instruction = instruction;
      this.Robot = robot;
    }

    public string Instruction { get; set; }
    public string Robot { get; set; }
  }
}
```

Note   The class requires a public constructor with no arguments so the serializer can instantiate it.

Now we can modify the RobotGrain to publish change events by pushing instances of this class onto a stream for every time an instruction is dequeued.

OrleansBook.GrainClasses/RobotGrain.cs

```
using System;
using System.Threading.Tasks;
using Microsoft.Extensions.Logging;
using Orleans;
using Orleans.Runtime;
using Orleans.Streams;
using OrleansBook.GrainInterfaces;

namespace OrleansBook.GrainClasses
{
  public class RobotGrain : Grain, IRobotGrain
  {
    ILogger<RobotGrain> logger;
    IPersistentState<RobotState> state;
    string key;
    IAsyncStream<InstructionMessage> stream;
```

```csharp
public RobotGrain(
  ILogger<RobotGrain> logger,
  [PersistentState("robotState", "robotStateStore")]
  IPersistentState<RobotState> state)
{
  this.logger = logger;
  this.state = state;
  this.key = this.GetPrimaryKeyString();
  this.stream = this
    .GetStreamProvider("SMSProvider")
    .GetStream<InstructionMessage>(
      Guid.Empty, "StartingInstruction");
}

Task Publish(string instruction)
{
  var message = new InstructionMessage(
    instruction, key);

  return this.stream.OnNextAsync(message);
}

public async Task AddInstruction(string instruction)
{
  var key = this.GetPrimaryKeyString();
  this.logger.LogWarning("{Key} returning '{Instruction}'",
    this.key, instruction);
  this.state.State.Instructions.Enqueue(instruction);
  await this.state.WriteStateAsync();
}

public Task<int> GetInstructionCount()
{
  return Task.FromResult(this.state.State.Instructions.Count);
}
```

```
    public async Task<string> GetNextInstruction()
    {
      if (this.state.State.Instructions.Count == 0)
      {
        return null;
      }

      var instruction = this.state.State.Instructions.Dequeue();
      var key = this.GetPrimaryKeyString();

      this.logger.LogWarning("{Key} returning '{Instruction}'",
        this.key, instruction);

      await this.Publish(instruction);

      await this.state.WriteStateAsync();
      return instruction;
    }
  }
}
```

The `OnActivate` method calls the `GetStreamProvider` method on the grains base class. The name of the stream provider must match that used in the `HostBuilder` configuration.

We use the stream provider to create the stream we're going to publish the event on. Streams are identified using a combination of a GUID and a namespace. In this example, we're using an empty GUID, and using one stream called "StartingInstruction," to indicate this is a stream for all robots starting an instruction.

Note   Streaming in Orleans is optimized for lots of transient streams. For example, we could have several streams for each grains, and like grains, the streams are virtual and effectively already exist before you write to them or read messages from them.

To actually add the message to the stream, we call `OnNextAsync`.

Subscribing to Streams in Grains

Grains can subscribe to streams. Any grains can subscribe to any stream at any time, but there is also the ability to have Orleans automatically activate a grains when a message appears on a stream. This is done using the [ImplicitStreamSubscription("STRE AM_NAMESPACE")] attribute. A grains class with this attribute will be activated (if it isn't already) with an ID matching the GUID of the stream for the given namespace.

We can implement this grains, first of all by adding an interface for it. Let's create a new interface in the OrleansBook.GrainInterfaces project:

OrleansBook.GrainInterfaces/ISubscriberGrain.cs

```
using Orleans;

namespace OrleansBook.GrainInterfaces
{
  public interface ISubscriberGrain: IGrainWithGuidKey
  { }
}
```

This interface does not have any public members, as this grains will not be addressed from the client and will be called exclusively by the stream.

The IGrainWithGuidKey interface is used, so the grains activations will have a GUID identity matching the GUID used for the stream. In our case, we just use an empty GUID, so there will be only one activation. We are introducing a bottleneck in the system by doing this, which is an anti-pattern, but we'll address this in a later chapter when it comes to optimization.

Note   Even though the interface is completely empty, it is still a requirement for a grains to have an interface.

We can then create the implementation for this grains in the OrleansBook. GrainClasses project.

OrleansBook.GrainClasses/SubscriberGrain.cs

```csharp
using System;
using System.Threading.Tasks;
using Orleans;
using Orleans.Streams;
using OrleansBook.GrainInterfaces;

namespace OrleansBook.GrainClasses
{
  [ImplicitStreamSubscription("StartingInstruction")]
  public class SubscriberGrain : Grain,
    ISubscriberGrain,
    IAsyncObserver<InstructionMessage>
  {
    public override async Task OnActivateAsync()
    {
      var key = this.GetPrimaryKey();

      await GetStreamProvider("SMSProvider")
        .GetStream<InstructionMessage>(key,
          "StartingInstruction")
        .SubscribeAsync(this);

      await base.OnActivateAsync();
    }

    public Task OnNextAsync(
      InstructionMessage instruction,
      StreamSequenceToken token = null)
    {
      var msg = $"{instruction.Robot} starting
        \"{instruction.Instruction}\"";
      Console.WriteLine(msg);
      return Task.CompletedTask;
    }

    public Task OnCompletedAsync() =>
      Task.CompletedTask;
```

```
    public Task OnErrorAsync(System.Exception ex) =>
      Task.CompletedTask;
  }
}
```

The grains is activated when a message appears on the stream, using the same GUID identity as the stream, but to actually retrieve the message, the grains must subscribe to the stream. This is done in the OnActivateAsync method, which is called immediately after grains activation.

Note   Constructors in C# cannot be async, so OnActivateAsync allows us to put async initialization code, such as subscribing to a stream or loading some initial state.

A reference to the stream is obtained in exactly the same way the RobotGrain does. The difference in this case is that the SubscribeAsync method is called, which requires an instance of IAsyncObserver<T>. In this case, we make the grains itself implement this interface and pass the grains in as the observer. This requires the grains to implement methods in response to stream events:

- **OnNextAsync** is the method called when a message is delivered to the subscriber. This happens after the publisher calls OnNextAsync. The message is passed as the first argument; an optional second argument "token" can be provided by the publisher to indicate message ordering.

- **OnCompletedAsync** is called when the publisher calls OnCompletedAsync on the stream. This indicates that the stream has closed and no further messages will be sent. In our example, we don't implement this.

- **OnErrorAsync** is used by Orleans to send error reports to the subscriber.

- An optional second argument "token" which the publisher can add. This is used to order the stream messages if required.

Running the OrleansBook.Host and OrleansBook.WebApi projects in the console and using cURL to update the values in the RobotGrain will result in the subscriber grains being activated on the host and writing out the changes to the console.

To create an instruction, use this command:

```
curl --request POST \
  --url http://localhost:5000/robot/Robbie/instruction \
  --header 'Content-Type: application/json' \
  --data '{
    "Value": "Do the dishes"
}'
```

To start an instruction, use this command:

```
curl --request GET \
  --url http://localhost:5000/robot/dave/instruction
```

You will then see this output on the Silos Host.

```
Robbie starting "Do the dishes"
```

Streams in the Client

The Client can also work with streams. A client can publish message and subscribe to streams.

This should first be configured in the ClientBuilder using the AddSimpleMessageStreamProvider extension method.

```
var client = new ClientBuilder()
  .UseLocalhostClustering()
  .AddSimpleMessageStreamProvider("SMSProvider")
  .Build();
```

Once the client has connected, we can use it to get a reference to the stream and either publish or subscribe to message in the same way the grains do.

For this example, we'll subscribe to the Delta stream in the OrleansBook.WebApi client project and write out to the console.

```
await client
  .GetStreamProvider("SMSProvider")
  .GetStream<Delta<StorageValue>>(Guid.Empty, "
    StartingInstruction ")
  .SubscribeAsync(new StreamSubscriber());
```

In this case, we create a class that implements IAsyncObserver<T> to handle the stream events in the same way the SubscriberGrain does.

```csharp
using System;
using System.Threading.Tasks;
using Orleans.Streams;

namespace OrleansBook.GrainInterfaces
{
  public class StreamSubscriber :
    IAsyncObserver<InstructionMessage>
  {
    public Task OnCompletedAsync()
    {
      Console.WriteLine("Completed");
      return Task.CompletedTask;
    }

    public Task OnErrorAsync(Exception ex)
    {
      Console.WriteLine("Exception");
      Console.WriteLine(ex.ToString());
      return Task.CompletedTask;
    }

    public Task OnNextAsync(
      InstructionMessage instruction,
      StreamSequenceToken token = null)
    {
      var msg = $"{instruction.Robot} starting \"{instruction.
      Instruction}\"";
```

```
    Console.WriteLine(msg);
    return Task.CompletedTask;
  }
 }
}
```

The Web API could respond to messages delivered by streams in many ways. Perhaps a call is made to a webhook, or a message is delivered in turn to a web socket. Streams allow us to build reactive applications and update the user immediately without resorting to polling.

Summary

Streams are an incredibly powerful concept, allowing us to decouple our application and focus on a message passing–based design.

The underlying implementation for a stream is abstracted away in Orleans, allowing us to support different stream providers without changing code.

Grains can be automatically activated in response to messages being delivered on streams. Streams in Orleans are designed to be transient. In the same way grains are virtual, streams also are virtual and do not require explicit creation.

Clients can both publish messages and subscribe to streams, making them a first-class participant.

Timers and Reminders

So far, we have seen grains being called by a client, and in response to messages in streams, but in some cases, we want to run code on a regular basis, perhaps every few seconds or minutes to support polling or a refresh. Perhaps we want to schedule code to be executed at a particular time in the future.

To address these requirements, Orleans supports Timers and Reminders.

In this chapter, we'll use a timer to collect reads and writes to the cache grains.

Timers vs. Reminders

Timers and Reminders have the same API and are used in a similar way, but have slightly different underlying semantics:

- **Timers** are for high-frequency regular calls while the grains is activated. They stop firing when the grains deactivates.

- **Reminders** are for low-frequency calls. A Reminder is persisted to storage and will activate the grains if the grains is not already active.

Both Timers and Reminders result in a method being called on the grains. This will be executed with the same turn-based concurrency of regular grains calls.

Registering a Timer

Timers are registered using the `RegisterTimer` method on the Grains base class with the parameters:

- **Callback**: The method to call when the timer fires.

- **State**: An object that can be passed to the timer. This may be useful when using multiple timers and a single callback method, but it can be left as null otherwise.

© Richard Astbury 2022
R. Astbury, *Microsoft Orleans for Developers*, https://doi.org/10.1007/978-1-4842-8167-3_10

- **DueTime**: The timespan before the timer first fires.

- **Period**: The timespan between timer callbacks.

The method returns an IDisposable which you can call Dispose() when you want to clear the timer. The timer will automatically stop when the grains deactivates.

For example, a timer is registered like this:

```
var oneMinute = TimeSpan.FromMinutes(1);
var timer = this.RegisterTimer(this.Callback, state, oneMinute, oneMinute);
```

The callback method then gets called every minute:

```
Task ResetStats(object _)
{
  Console.WriteLine("Callback");
  return Task.CompletedTask;
}
```

Adding a Timer to the RobotGrain

It's nice to know how productive your robot is and whether it's undertaking tasks or just sitting around reading the paper. We'll record the number of tasks performed, during the time the grains is activated, and keep a track of tasks per minute. This means we need to reset the counters every minute, which requires a timer.

We will modify the RobotGrain to register a timer when it activates. When the timer fires, the grains will write out the stats to the console and reset the counters.

```
using System;
using System.Threading.Tasks;
using Microsoft.Extensions.Logging;
using Orleans;
using Orleans.Runtime;
using OrleansBook.GrainInterfaces;

namespace OrleansBook.GrainClasses
{
  public class RobotGrain : Grain, IRobotGrain
  {
```

```
int instructionsEnqueued = 0;
int instructionsDequeued = 0;
ILogger<RobotGrain> logger;
IPersistentState<RobotState> state;

public RobotGrain(
  ILogger<RobotGrain> logger,
  [PersistentState("robotState", "robotStateStore")]
  IPersistentState<RobotState> state)
{
  this.logger = logger;
  this.state = state;
}

Task Publish(string instruction)
{
  var message = new InstructionMessage(
    instruction,
    this.GetPrimaryKeyString());

  return this
    .GetStreamProvider("SMSProvider")
    .GetStream<InstructionMessage>(Guid.Empty, "StartingInstruction")
    .OnNextAsync(message);
}

public async Task AddInstruction(string instruction)
{
  var key = this.GetPrimaryKeyString();
  this.logger.LogWarning($"{key} adding '{instruction}'");
  this.state.State.Instructions.Enqueue(instruction);
  this.instructionsEnqueued += 1;
  await this.state.WriteStateAsync();
}

public Task<int> GetInstructionCount()
{
  return
```

```
      Task.FromResult(this.state.State.Instructions.Count);
}

public async Task<string> GetNextInstruction()
{
  if (this.state.State.Instructions.Count == 0)
  {
    return null;
  }

  var instruction = this.state.State.Instructions.Dequeue();
  var key = this.GetPrimaryKeyString();

  this.logger.LogWarning(
    $"{key} returning '{instruction}'");

  await this.Publish(instruction);
  this.instructionsDequeued += 1;
  await this.state.WriteStateAsync();
  return instruction;
}

public override Task OnActivateAsync()
{
  var oneMinute = TimeSpan.FromMinutes(1);
  this.RegisterTimer(
    this.ResetStats, null, oneMinute, oneMinute);
  return base.OnActivateAsync();
}

Task ResetStats(object _)
{
  var key = this.GetPrimaryKeyString();

  Console.WriteLine(
    $"{key} enqueued: {this.instructionsEnqueued}");
  Console.WriteLine(
    $"{key} dequeued: {this.instructionsDequeued}");
```

```
    Console.WriteLine(
      $"{key} queued: {this.state.State.Instructions.Count}");

    this.instructionsEnqueued = 0;
    this.instructionsDequeued = 0;

    return Task.CompletedTask;
  }
 }
}
```

Note   The Console is not really the right place to publish this data, but we're keeping this example as simple as possible to demonstrate the concepts.

We add the OnActivateAsync method override to the grains as a place to register the timer. The ResetStats method is called on a one minute interval to write the stats out and then reset the counters. Note that the counters are member variables and not part of the state object, as we can treat them as volatile state that doesn't need to be persisted.

When running the Host and Web API projects, now you will see each active grains write out the statistics to the console.

```
Robbie enqueued: 2
Robbie dequeued: 1
Robbie queued: 1
```

Adding a Reminder to the RobotGrain

In order to keep the robot up to date, we need to remind it to check if there are any firmware updates. This is a daily task, so we'll add an instruction once per day to remind the robot to do a check.

We can use a reminder for this. The reminder will fire on a 24 hour schedule and add a task to the robot's list. A reminder will activate the grains if it isn't already active.

Reminders require a data store so they can be persisted. This needs to be configured in the Host. For development, there is a UseInMemoryReminderService extension method on SiloHostBuilder to add an in-memory store. We'll use this for convenience. Of course, our reminders will not persist after restarting the Host, but that's ok for development.

The host configuration should now look like this:

```
using System;
using System.Threading.Tasks;
using Microsoft.Extensions.Logging;
using Orleans;
using Orleans.Hosting;
using Orleans.Statistics;
using OrleansBook.GrainClasses;

namespace OrleansBook.Host
{
  class Program
  {
    static async Task Main()
    {
      var host = new SiloHostBuilder()
        .ConfigureApplicationParts(parts => parts.AddApplicationPart(typeof
        (ExampleGrain).Assembly).WithReferences())
        .UseLocalhostClustering()
        .ConfigureLogging(logging =>
        {
          logging.AddConsole();
          logging.SetMinimumLevel(LogLevel.Information);
        })
        .UseDashboard()
        .UseLinuxEnvironmentStatistics()
        .AddMemoryGrainStorageAsDefault()
        .AddMemoryGrainStorage("PubSubStore")
        .AddSimpleMessageStreamProvider("SMSProvider")
        .UseInMemoryReminderService()
        .Build();

      await host.StartAsync();

      Console.WriteLine("Press enter to stop the Silo...");
      Console.ReadLine();
```

```
      await host.StopAsync();
    }
  }
}
```

To register a reminder, we call the `RegisterOrUpdateReminder` method. This has three parameters and is similar to the Timer:

- **ReminderName**: A grains can have multiple reminders, so a name allows us to set and respond to them separately.

- **DueTime**: The timespan before the reminder fires.

- **Period**: The timespan between reminder calls.

Unlike the timer, the reminder does not require a method that gets called back or a state that is passed to this method. Instead, the grains must implement the `IRemindable` interface, which adds a `ReceiveReminder` method to the grains. This method will be called when the reminder fires.

Note   If the grains is not activated when the reminder fires, the `OnActivateAsync` method will be called first, followed by the `ReceiveReminder` method.

OrleansBook.GrainClasses/RobotGrain.cs

```
public async override Task OnActivateAsync()
{
  var oneMinute = TimeSpan.FromMinutes(1);
  this.RegisterTimer(
    this.ResetStats, null, oneMinute, oneMinute);

  var oneDay = TimeSpan.FromDays(1);
  await RegisterOrUpdateReminder("firmware", oneDay, oneDay);

  await base.OnActivateAsync();
}
```

In this example, we call the reminder "firmware" and use a timespan and period of one day. If we have previously set a reminder of this name, it will be overwritten.

Note   The OnActivateAsync method is now marked as async. The RegisterOrUpdateReminder method is async as it writes the reminder to a storage system.

We can now implement the ReceiveReminder method. In our case, this will add an instruction to the robot's queue of instructions.

OrleansBook.GrainClasses/RobotGrain.cs

```
public Task ReceiveReminder(string reminderName, Orleans.Runtime.
TickStatus status)
{
  if (reminderName == "firmware")
    return this.AddInstruction("Update firmware");
  return Task.CompletedTask;
}
```

Summary

In this chapter, we compared Timers and Reminders. Both have a similar API and behavior, allowing you to register grains methods to be called in the future at a given frequency. While both of these features are similar, they have different purposes. A Timer is for high-frequency calls while the grains is active. A Reminder is designed to activate a grains over a longer period. Of course, these two concepts can be mixed, so you can explore the advantages of both.

CHAPTER 11

Transactions

In this chapter, we will learn how Orleans supports transactions across grains. This allows us to update the state of multiple grains in one atomic operation to avoid scenarios where failure can lead to inconsistent state across grains.

Motivation for Transactions

Transactions are useful when a system has distributed state that is co-dependent. Using payments as an example, if the amount was deducted from one account but not credited to the second, perhaps due to a transient fault, we would see an inconsistent state and unhappy customers.

In conventional system architectures, transactions are typically supplied by the database. In many architectures, it is desirable to support more than one kind of database, but as transactions are typically scoped to a single database, we can only provide transactional guarantees within that scope.

There are many possible solutions to work around these problems, but Orleans provides the option to elevate the transaction concept into the application tier. This means that the underlying data store does not need to provide transaction support, allowing us to choose a cheaper or more scalable service.

Orleans uses a novel variation of the two-phase commit in an attempt to provide distributed transaction without the performance penalty. You can read more about it in the paper from Microsoft Research (`www.microsoft.com/en-us/research/wp-content/uploads/2016/10/EldeebBernstein-TransactionalActors-MSR-TR-1.pdf`).

© Richard Astbury 2022

R. Astbury, *Microsoft Orleans for Developers*, https://doi.org/10.1007/978-1-4842-8167-3_11

What Is ACID?

Orleans' transactions are ACID compliant. ACID is an acronym of a set of guarantees that a system can provide:

- **Atomicity**: The operation either completely succeeds or completely fails. It will be rolled back to its previous state if it is unsuccessful.

- **Consistency**: The data will always have integrity and will not be left in an incorrect state.

- **Isolation**: Updates in one transaction will not be impacted by reads or writes in another transaction.

- **Durability**: Successful transactions will be persisted permanently.

A database transaction is ACID compliant when it keeps these guarantees while it makes updates to multiple records.

Creating an Azure Storage Account

Transactions require storage, and the memory-based storage used so far in this book does not support Transactions. A Microsoft Azure–based Transaction storage library is available, so we'll use that.

You will need a Microsoft Azure account, with a Storage Account. If you already have one, you can skip these steps and use your existing storage keys. Otherwise, read on and we'll create a new one.

The Storage Account is not likely to cost more than a few cents.

You can create a Storage Account in the Azure portal or the Azure CLI. Following are the commands to create it with the CLI. The instructions on getting started with the CLI are here: `https://docs.microsoft.com/en-us/cli/azure/get-started-with-azure-cli`.

Once you have signed up, you can create a resource group, and then a storage account, where you should replace `MY_STORAGE_NAME` with your own unique name in lower case.

```
az group create --location westus --resource-group OrleansBook
```

```
az storage account create -n MY_STORAGE_NAME -g OrleansBook -l westus --sku
Standard_LRS
```

```
az storage account keys list --account-name MY_STORAGE_NAME
```

The final command retrieves the connection string information. You should see some output like this:

```
[
  {
    "keyName": "key1",
    "permissions": "FULL",
    "value": "MY_STORAGE_KEY"
  },
  {
    "keyName": "key2",
    "permissions": "FULL",
    "value": " MY_STORAGE_KEY "
  }
]
```

To create the connection string, replace the MY_STORAGE_NAME and MY_STORAGE_KEY with the values you got from the preceding steps:

```
AccountName=MY_STORAGE_NAME;AccountKey=MY_STORAGE_KEY
```

Configuring Transactions

Transactions are provided via an additional NuGet package. Grains are required to be specifically written to take advantage of transactions, so rewrite the internals of our Robot grains, but still support the same robot functionality and interface. We'll also add a new grains type which will take a number of instructions and distribute these to various robots in the same transaction scope.

First, let's add the required NuGet packages to the Host.

```
cd OrleansBook.Host
dotnet add package Microsoft.Orleans.Transactions
dotnet add package Microsoft.Orleans.Transactions.AzureStorage
```

We can then configure the host using extension methods on the HostBuilder in Program.cs.

OrleansBook/Host/Program.cs

```
var host = new SiloHostBuilder()
  .AddAzureTableTransactionalStateStorage(
    "TransactionStore",
    o => o.ConnectionString =
      "AccountName=MY_STORAGE_NAME;AccountKey=MY_STORAGE_KEY"
  })
  .UseTransactions()
  .Build();
```

You will need to substitute the MY_STORAGE_NAME and MY_STORAGE_KEY with your own Azure Storage credentials.

Note   The other configuration methods have been omitted for brevity.

Grains Interfaces

We'll introduce a new grains interface to support transactions. The IBatchGrain will take a batch of updates and call the AddInstruction method on IRobotGrain for each of the instructions in the batch.

The AddInstructions method on the batch grains will take an array of (string, string) tuples, representing the key-value pairs we want to store.

OrleansBook.GrainInterfaces/IBatchGrain.cs

```
using System;
using System.Threading.Tasks;
using Orleans;

namespace OrleansBook.GrainInterfaces
{
  public interface IBatchGrain : IGrainWithIntegerKey
  {
```

```
    [Transaction(TransactionOption.Create)]
    Task AddInstructions((string,string)[] values);
  }
}
```

The important feature here is the attribute decorating the AddInstructions method. The Transaction attribute declares how this method contributes to Transactions. In this case, it creates a transaction. There are a few choices under the TransactionOption enum:

- **Create**: Calls to this method will start a new transaction, even if the call chain already has a transaction open.

- **Join**: The method is transactional but can only be called within an open transaction.

- **CreateOrJoin**: The method is transactional and will either join an existing open transaction or create a new one.

- **Suppress**: The method will not participate in a transaction but can be called from within an open transaction. It will not receive the transaction context.

- **Supported**: The method will not participate in a transaction but can be called from within an open transaction. It will receive the transaction context.

- **NotAllowed**: The method does not support transactions and cannot be called from within a transaction. It will throw a NotSupportedException in this case.

The IRobotGrain interface will also carry these attributes, but will otherwise remain unchanged.

OrleansBook.GrainInterfaces/IRobotGrain.cs

```
using System;
using System.Threading.Tasks;
using Orleans;

namespace OrleansBook.GrainInterfaces
{
  public interface IRobotGrain: IGrainWithStringKey
```

```
  {
    [Transaction(TransactionOption.CreateOrJoin)]
    Task AddInstruction(string instruction);

    [Transaction(TransactionOption.CreateOrJoin)]
    Task<string> GetNextInstruction();

    [Transaction(TransactionOption.CreateOrJoin)]
    Task<int> GetInstructionCount();
  }
}
```

All methods use the TransactionOption.CreateOrJoin attribute; even though only the AddInstruction method will alter the state, they all read the state and therefore need to participate in the transaction.

Implementing Grains Classes

The implementation of the IBatchGrain interface requires us to provide a method which will call out to IRobotGrain instances for each key-value pair provided.

OrleansBook.GrainClasses/BatchGrain.cs

```
using System.Linq;
using System.Threading.Tasks;
using Orleans;
using Orleans.Concurrency;
using OrleansBook.GrainInterfaces;

namespace OrleansBook.GrainClasses
{
  [StatelessWorker]
  public class BatchGrain : Grain, IBatchGrain
  {
    public Task AddInstructions((string,string)[] values)
    {
      var tasks = values.Select(keyValue =>
        this.GrainFactory
```

```
        .GetGrain<IRobotGrain>(keyValue.Item1)
        .AddInstruction(keyValue.Item2)
    );

    return Task.WhenAll(tasks);
    }
  }
}
```

It's worth noting a couple of optimizations here. The first is to use `Task.WhenAll` to await all the grains calls together, rather than making the calls sequentially. This parallelizes the calls to `IRobotGrain`, reducing the overall latency for this request. This pattern is called an async fan-out.

The second is that this grains doesn't use any aspect of its identity, and in fact just having a single activation of it would be suboptimal and present a bottleneck in our system. To address this, we add the `StatelessWorker` attribute. This permits Orleans to create multiple activations of this grains instead of queueing messages to a single instance. The grains will still have the single-threaded guarantees, but there could be several copies of it in every silos.

We'll simplify the implementation of the `RobotGrain` and remove the streams, timers, and reminders and focus on the transactional state.

OrleansBook.GrainClasses/RobotGrain.cs

```
using System;
using System.Threading.Tasks;
using Microsoft.Extensions.Logging;
using Orleans;
using Orleans.Transactions.Abstractions;
using OrleansBook.GrainInterfaces;

namespace OrleansBook.GrainClasses
{
  public class RobotGrain : Grain, IRobotGrain
  {
    ILogger<RobotGrain> logger;
    ITransactionalState<RobotState> state;

    public RobotGrain(
```

```
    ILogger<RobotGrain> logger,
    [TransactionalState("robotState", "robotStateStore")]
    ITransactionalState<RobotState> state)
{
  this.logger = logger;
  this.state = state;
}

public async Task AddInstruction(string instruction)
{
  var key = this.GetPrimaryKeyString();
  this.logger.LogWarning($"{key} adding '{instruction}'");
  await this.state.PerformUpdate(state =>
    state.Instructions.Enqueue(instruction));
}

public async Task<int> GetInstructionCount()
{
  return await this.state.PerformRead(
    state => state.Instructions.Count);
}

public async Task<string> GetNextInstruction()
{
  var key = this.GetPrimaryKeyString();
  string instruction = null;
  await this.state.PerformUpdate(state =>
  {
    if (state.Instructions.Count == 0) return;
    instruction = state.Instructions.Dequeue();
  });

  if (null != instruction)
  {
    this.logger.LogWarning(
      $"{key} returning '{instruction}'");
  }
```

```
    return instruction;
  }
 }
}
```

Instead of using the persistence model used in earlier chapters, we use the ITransactionalState<T> interface. This is also a service passed in on the constructor. Similarly, the parameter needs to be marked with the TransactionalState custom attribute to indicate the name of the store and storage provider. Like the persistent state, we can have multiple states with different providers if required.

In our case, we only have a member variable "state," and we'll use the default transaction store "robotStateStore."

When dealing with state, instead of altering the state directly, the variable has the methods PerformRead and PerformUpdate, both of which expect a synchronous function which reads or updates the states, respectively. This allows the transaction system to apply or cancel these operations transactionally.

Note   There is no explicit "commit" or "rollback" with Orleans Transactions. State is rolled back in the event of an exception being thrown somewhere in the call chain.

Adding a Controller

We'll create a new "batch" controller to call the new grains we have created.

   OrleansBook.WebApi/BatchController.cs

```
using System;
using Orleans;
using System.Threading.Tasks;
using Microsoft.AspNetCore.Mvc;
using OrleansBook.GrainInterfaces;
using System.Collections.Generic;
using System.Linq;

namespace OrleansBook.WebApi.Controllers
```

```
{
  [ApiController]
  public class BatchController : ControllerBase
  {
    private readonly IClusterClient _client;

    public BatchController(IClusterClient client) =>
      _client = client;

    [HttpPost]
    [Route("batch")]
    public async Task<IActionResult>
Post(IDictionary<string,string> values)
    {
      var grain = this._client.GetGrain<IBatchGrain>(0);

      var input = values
        .Select(keyValue => (keyValue.Key, keyValue.Value))
        .ToArray();

      await grain.AddInstructions(input);

      return Ok();
    }
  }
}
```

This controller is similar to RobotController, in that it takes an IClusterClient as a parameter on the constructor.

The Post method expects a JSON object in the body. It converts this into an array of key-value pair tuples, which it then sends to the BatchGrain. The batch grains is a stateless worker, so the identity of it can be anything. We're using zero.

When we start the host and the Web API projects, we can try out our new transaction.

To post a batch of values:

```
curl \
  --header "Content-Type: application/json" \
  --request POST \
```

```
--data '{"hal": "Open the doors", "rob": "Make the tea"}' \
http://localhost:5000/batch
```

To read a value:

```
curl http://localhost:5000/batch/
```

Returns:

```
Value1
```

Summary

We've seen how Orleans allows us to incorporate transactions as a feature of our application code, rather than being something we rely on our database to do. This means we can use data stores with a more basic set of guarantees, such as Azure Storage, which in theory should allow us to store data at a higher throughput than a conventional database.

Transactions are useful when we have items of data that are dependent upon each other, such as exchanging currency in a game, allowing us to avoid inconsistent state.

CHAPTER 12

Event Sourced Grains

Overview

The state of a grains is typically a single data structure. The grains will mutate the fields over time and persist when appropriate. Orleans provides an alternative way of managing state. Instead of a single data structure, we can consider state as the accumulation of a number of events which, applied in sequence, generates the state object. We call this event sourcing.

In this chapter, we will see how Orleans natively supports event sourcing, by creating a journaled grains which has a state log rather than a single value for state.

Introducing Event Sourcing

We often think about state as a single data structure, such as a record in a database, which we continually update to represent the real world. However, if you consider scenarios like a bank account, your balance isn't really a single record, but the result of your entire transaction history with various debits and credits over time. There are some great advantages to this approach: You can replay or even reverse events, making some debugging and bug-fixing scenarios easier. You also get an audit log of every action performed on an entity.

Event sourced grains are an optional feature you can choose to include. Let's create a simple one now.

© Richard Astbury 2022
R. Astbury, *Microsoft Orleans for Developers*, https://doi.org/10.1007/978-1-4842-8167-3_12

Defining the State

We will start our implementation by modeling the state or rather thinking about the events that will mutate the state.

OrleansBook.GrainClasses/Events.cs

```
using System;

namespace OrleansBook.GrainClasses
{
  public interface IEvent
  { }

  public class EnqueueEvent : IEvent
  {
    public string Value { get; }
    public EnqueueEvent() { }
    public EnqueueEvent(string value) =>
      this.Value = value;
  }

  public class DequeueEvent : IEvent
  {
    public string Value { get; set; }
    public DequeueEvent() { }
  }
}
```

Here, we define an interface that represents an event, which our state will eventually respond to. We don't need any public members on the interface; it's just used to indicate which objects we want to use as events.

We have two classes that implement the interface and represent events in the system. The EnqueueEvent represents a new instruction to be given to the robot; the DequeueEvent represents an instruction to be retrieved. These classes do not perform these updates; they are purely signals, only holding the necessary data required to complete the state mutation (in this case, the value is the instruction).

These classes must be serializable, hence the parameterless constructor.

OrleansBook.GrainClasses/EventSourcedState.cs

```csharp
using System;
using System.Collections.Generic;

namespace OrleansBook.GrainClasses
{
  public class EventSourcedState
  {
    Queue<string> instructions = new Queue<string>();

    public int Count => this.instructions.Count;

    public void Apply(EnqueueEvent @event) =>
      this.instructions.Enqueue(@event.Value);

    public void Apply(DequeueEvent @event)
    {
      if (this.instructions.Count == 0) return;
      @event.Value = this.instructions.Dequeue();
    }
  }
}
```

We now create a class which will maintain the current value of the state by applying the events. The EventSourcedState class has a private member instructions which holds the current queue of instructions for the robot. Overloaded Apply methods then mutate that queue according to the type of event. In this way, we can support many types of events, and as the classes are all Plain Old CLR Objects (POCOs), it's easy to test this behavior with unit tests.

Implementing the Grains Class

We can use the existing IRobotGrain interface, as it is only the implementation of the grains we wish to change. Event sourcing does provide us with the additional capability of querying the history of events, which we could expose on this interface, but to keep things simple, we won't.

To implement an event sourced grains, we need to add a reference to the Microsoft. Orleans.EventSourcing NuGet package.

```
cd OrleansBook.GrainClasses
dotnet add reference Microsoft.Orleans.EventSourcing
```

This package adds a JournaledGrain base class that our grains will inherit from instead of Grain.

We can then implement our interface as follows:

OrleansBook.GrainClasses/EventSourcedGrain.cs

```
using System;
using System.Threading.Tasks;
using OrleansBook.GrainInterfaces;
using Orleans.EventSourcing;
using Orleans.Providers;

namespace OrleansBook.GrainClasses
{
  [StorageProvider(ProviderName = "robotStateStore")]
  public class EventSourcedGrain : JournaledGrain<EventSourcedState,
IEvent>, IRobotGrain
  {
    public async Task AddInstruction(string instruction)
    {
      RaiseEvent(new EnqueueEvent(instruction));
      await ConfirmEvents();
    }

    public async Task<string> GetNextInstruction()
    {
      if (this.State.Count == 0) return null;

      var @event = new DequeueEvent();
      RaiseEvent(@event);
      await ConfirmEvents();
      return @event.Value;
    }
```

```
    public Task<int> GetInstructionCount()
        => Task.FromResult(this.State.Count);
  }
}
```

There are a few things to note in the implementation. We must specify the storage provider we want to use using the `StorageProvider` attribute on the class, we can reuse the memory provider configured in previous chapter, so no need to modify the host configuration.

The class itself derives from `JournaledGrain<TGrainState, TEventBase>` where `TGrainState` is the `EventSourcedState` class and `TEventBase` is the `IEvent` interface. The grains also inherits from the `IRobotGrain` interface as you would expect.

Note   It is not strictly necessary to provide the `TEventBase` generic parameter, and it will default to being object. But in our case, it provides `IEvent` type constraint to the `RaiseEvent` method, making it a little clearer to the developer.

JournaledGrain provides two methods for updating the state: `RaiseEvent` and `ConfirmEvents`.

Our grains calls these in turn. `RaiseEvent` applies the new event to the current state (e.g., we could be applying a credit to the account balance; this would adjust the current balance value). We can call multiple times `RaiseEvent` within the grains logic. The updates are only applied in memory.

When we call `RaiseEvent`, the `Apply` method on the `EventSourcedState` object we defined earlier is called. The appropriate overload being called for the given event.

We then call `ConfirmEvents` to persist these events to the underlying storage. This method should be called before the method returns to ensure the events are committed to storage.

Note   The calls to `RaiseEvent` are synchronous and will only mutate the local state; calls to `ConfirmEvents` are asynchronous, as it makes the call to storage.

The implementation of the underlying storage provider determines how the grains state is generated on activation. If the storage provider records all of the events, it presents these all to the grains on activation. Each of these events will be replayed in turn, resulting in the state being regenerated. Alternatively, some storage providers will only present the latest version of the state, in which case this replay process does not occur.

The GetInstructionCount method requires the current number of instructions in the queue. As the EventSourcedState class maintains the current state, it's able to provide this information without deferring to the storage provider or replaying any of the events. It's a feature of the in-memory state.

As well as providing a property for State, the JournaledGrain also has a Version property. This is the number of confirmed events the grains has received. The value starts at zero and is automatically incremented after each successful state operation.

The grains can also access the history of confirmed events using the RetrieveConfirmedEvents method. This async method accepts a range of versions as arguments and will return the corresponding events as an IEnumerable.

```
var events = await this.RetrieveConfirmedEvents(0, this.Version);
```

This allows you to scan through the events that have been applied to provide an audit log or similar.

Note   At the time of writing, the RetrieveConfirmedEvents method throws a not supported exception, because the in-memory storage does not support retrieving the log history.

Adding the Controller

As the event sourced grains provides the same behavior as its regular counterpart, it is not necessary to make any significant changes to the controller. We do however now have two grains with the same interface. As the grains client uses the interface to distinguish which grains type to send a message to, we need to provide a hint to the Orleans to use our new version instead of the old. We can do this by providing a value for the grainClassNamePrefix argument:

OrleansBook.WebApi/Controllers/RobotController.cs

```
var grain = this._client.GetGrain<IRobotGrain>(
  name,
  "OrleansBook.GrainClasses.EventSourcedGrain");
```

Only the calls to GetGrain need to be updated; the other lines of code can remain the same.

As before, we can use cURL to test the code.

To set a value, we can POST some JSON:

```
curl \
  --header "Content-Type: application/json" \
  --request POST \
  --data '{"Value": "Feed the dog"}' \
  http://localhost:5000/robot/daneel/instruction
```

We can then read that value with a GET:

```
curl http://localhost:5000/robot/daneel/instruction
```

This returns:

```
Feed the dog
```

Unconfirmed State

There may be a performance advantage in only saving state periodically, rather than after every event. To allow this, the Journaled Grains allows you to work with uncommitted state. This also affords you the flexibility to continue processing state changes while the underlying storage is undergoing an outage.

The TentativeState property provides the grains access to the current unconfirmed state.

The UnconfirmedEvents property provides an IEnumerable of the events that have not yet been committed to storage.

The OnStateChanged and OnTentativeStateChanged methods can be overridden, so you can respond to any change in state. Note that OnTentativeStateChanged will always be called when state is about to change. OnStateChanged will also be called when the write to storage is successful.

Summary

Event sourced grains provide an alternative approach to state, where state is a product of a series of events, rather than just a single value maintained by the grains.

There are some advantages to using this approach, such as having a built-in history of updates over time which can be replayed when the grains is activated, allowing bug fixes to be applied to events that occurred in the past.

CHAPTER 13

Updating Grains

Over time, we'll want to update our grains in response to new requirements or bug fixes; in this chapter, we'll discuss a few approaches to this and explore how to control the behavior of clusters containing a mixture of grains versions.

Updating Grains Logic

Updating the logic inside your grains is straightforward. Assuming that the grain's interface is unchanged and the old and new versions of the grains are compatible, you can upgrade the silos running in the cluster.

You can do this either by standing up a new "staging" environment, which you can then do a swap with the production environment, or you can incrementally upgrade each silos in turn by removing it from the cluster, upgrading the silos, and then joining it back to the cluster again.

Both strategies have their pros and cons. The staging environment allows you to test the new version before swapping it with production, However, if you just switch all traffic from one environment to the other, the new environment will have no active grains; there may be a performance penalty as every grains is reactivated. If it's possible to direct a percentage of traffic between the prod and staging environments, then you can slow down the switching time and mitigate this, although you may now find that you have grains instances in both environments.

The incremental approach allows you to upgrade silos in place, which means you can slowly roll out an update across the cluster, but it might require more development effort to build scripts to manage this process, including rolling back if a problem is encountered.

© Richard Astbury 2022
R. Astbury, *Microsoft Orleans for Developers*, https://doi.org/10.1007/978-1-4842-8167-3_13

Interface Versioning

What becomes more problematic is a rolling upgrade with a grains whose interface has changed. If we add a new method to a grains, we'll find ourselves in the situation that some activations in the cluster have the method and some don't. A call from a new grains to an old grains will result in an exception.

To help with this, Orleans allows us to annotate grains interfaces with a version number, by means of a Version attribute.

```
[Version(1)]
public interface IRobotGrain: IGrainWithStringKey
{
    ...
}
```

All grains have a version number. If the version isn't declared, it defaults to zero.

By default, Orleans assumes that grains are backward compatible, but not forward compatible. This assumption demands that you only make additions to grains interfaces. You should not remove methods from a grains interface or adjust method signatures. You should add entirely new methods instead.

When a request is sent, either by a grains or a client, the grains interface is used to create the call. The version information of the client is included in this call. The cluster will then send this request to the correct activation in the correct silos based on the grains identity. If the version of the activation is compatible (by default, this means that the version number is equal or greater), then the activation proceeds with handling the call as usual. If the version is incompatible (the version is lower), then grains is deactivated, and a compatible grains is activated in a compatible silos.

This behavior can be overridden when building the silos.

```
var silo = new SiloHostBuilder()
  .Configure<GrainVersioningOptions>(o =>
  {
    o.DefaultCompatibilityStrategy = nameof(BackwardCompatible);
    o.DefaultVersionSelectorStrategy = nameof(MinimumVersion);
  })
```

The DefaultCompatibilityStrategy property can be set to either of the following:

- **BackwardCompatible**: The default, which allows grains with a higher version to fulfill requests made with a lower version

- **AllVersionsCompatible**: Essentially disables the versioning constraints and allows calls between any versions

- **StrictVersionCompatible**: Requires the grains version to exactly match that of the request

The DefaultVersionSelectorStrategy property is used to select which compatible grains version should be created, in cases where a number of different versions are available in the cluster:

- **LatestVersion**: The greatest compatible grains version available in the cluster will be activated.

- **MinimumVersion**: The lowest compatible grains version will be activated.

- **AllCompatibleVersions**: The default, whereby any compatible grains version can be activated.

Interface versioning is not supported on Stateless Worker grains or streaming grains.

Upgrading State

When we make changes to the classes used to persist the grain's state, we must take care to ensure that any changes we make are backward compatible, by taking care to only add properties to the state class that are nullable and that the underlying storage provider is using a version-tolerant serializer, such as JSON.

If this is not the case, and we roll out an update to the grains where Orleans cannot deserialize an incompatible state, an exception will be thrown and the grains will not be activated.

There is no built-in support for versioning or upgrading state in Orleans.

Summary

There are benefits in incrementally rolling out updates to a cluster, allowing us to slowly transition from one version to the next, avoiding too much degradation in service. However, this brings some complexity when thinking about different versions of grains communicating with one another. We learnt in this chapter that the version attribute helps to control this, giving us predictable behavior during an upgrade.

In this chapter, we also mention that state should also be given consideration when updates are made to the system and that backward compatibility is required when making changes to the state classes.

CHAPTER 14

Optimization

We have covered all the basic features of Orleans, but to get some higher throughput for some scenarios, there are a few optimizations and advanced features we can take advantage of. Some of these optimizations affect the guarantees that Orleans offers, so they must be used with care as using a feature incorrectly may result in unpredictable behavior.

Stateless Workers

We already made use of Stateless Workers previously in this book, but for completeness, we'll include them here too.

Orleans guarantees that while under normal operation (i.e., while not undergoing a network partition), there will be a maximum of one activation of each grains.

In some cases, we may have a grains that does not have any internal state, and instead just processes some data, or handles requests to an external system. In this case, we can have multiple activations of the grains to avoid having a bottleneck in the system.

We do this by adding the [StatelessWorker] attribute to the grains class.

```
[StatelessWorker]
public class ExampleGrain : Grain, IExampleGrain
{
  ...
}
```

When Orleans sees this attribute instead of queueing messages for this grains, it will create another activation which will process the message.

Another advantage of Stateless Workers is they are always activated on the same Silos as the caller. This reduces the latency and overhead of making calls to them.

© Richard Astbury 2022
R. Astbury, *Microsoft Orleans for Developers*, https://doi.org/10.1007/978-1-4842-8167-3_14

While they don't have any persistable state, they can still maintain member variables in memory between calls and can therefore act as a scalable cache.

Stateless Worker activations are then subject to the same deactivation rules as normal grains and will be removed after they stop receiving messages.

Reentrancy

By default, grains process their message queues one message at a time. The next message is not picked up until the first has been completed. Reentrancy modifies this behavior allowing the grains to process the next message while it is awaiting a task, such as an I/O operation on the previous message. The calls to the grains are interleaved, the grains still only uses thread, but it provides the grains the opportunity to process something while awaiting.

Reentrancy can provide a grains, particularly one that highly contended, to be more efficient. The downside is that it may mean that when your code returns from an await operation, the member variables of the grains may have been modified by another call that was processed during the await.

There are three ways to enable reentrancy on a grains:

1. Add the [Reentrant] attribute to the grains class. This makes every method on the grains reentrant at all times.

2. Add the [AlwaysInterleave] attribute to an individual method on the grains interface. This marks a single method as reentrant, regardless of whether the grains is marked as Reentrant or not.

3. Add the [MayInterleave("MethodName")] attribute to the grains class. This allows you to provide the name of a static method on the grains class which accepts an InvokeMethodRequest as an argument,·and will return a true/false to enable/disable reentrancy dynamically, based on the method that will run, and/or the values of the arguments.

Cancellation Tokens

Orleans supports the cancellation of calls to grains with the GrainCancellationToken class, which is symmetrical to the CancellationToken found in the .NET.

```
// create the token
using var tcs = new GrainCancellationTokenSource();

// call the grain, pass it the token
await grain.DoSomething(tcs.Token);

// the call can be cancelled by calling Cancel
await tcs.Cancel();
```

Note   The GrainCancellationTokenSource should be disposed after use.

If the call to Cancel fails, due to a transient network error, an exception is thrown, and the call can be retried.

The grains code should check the cancellation token so it can avoid unnecessary processing if it has been cancelled.

```
public async Task DoSomething(GrainCancellationToken token)
{
  if (!token.CancellationToken.IsCancellationRequested)
  {
    // continue
  }
}
```

The cancellation token can be passed down a call chain to other grains if needed.

Cancellation tokens allow callers of grains to cancel grains calls to avoid unnecessary processing, which could provide some efficiency for long-running operations.

One-Way Requests

Orleans supports sending one-way messages to grains. This optimization avoids the need for a return message to be sent to the client, thus reducing network and serialization overheads.

This is achieved by adding the [OneWay] attribute to the method on the grains interface.

```
public interface IExampleGrain : IGrainWithGuidKey
{
  [OneWay]
  Task OneWayMethod(string value);
}
```

One-way methods can only return Task or ValueTask and not any associated data (i.e., Task<string> is not permitted).

When a call is made to a one-way method, the caller is not notified of the successful completion of the call. In fact, there is no guarantee that the grains received the message or that the method ran without exception. Therefore, this optimization should only be considered for noncritical notifications to the grains.

The following chapter covers another mechanism for sending notification messages, Observers, which allows you to make callbacks to grains or clients.

Readonly

If a grains method never modifies the state of a grains, for example, the method just returns the current value of the state, the grains method can be marked with the [Readonly] attribute. This allows Orleans to take a more efficient route through the code, which should provide slightly faster calls to this method.

```
public class ExampleGrain : Grain, IExampleGrain
{
  [Readonly]
  public Task<string> GetValue()
  {
    return "example";
  }
}
```

Immutable

When two grains are co-located in the same Silos, the objects they exchange through calling each other are not serialized over the network, but instead a deep copy of them is made. This ensures that one grains cannot inadvertently interfere with the internal state of any grains, by altering an object passed by reference.

Compared to making a network call, a local call is still considerably faster and more efficient, but a deep copy can be both computationally expensive and require memory allocations. If the caller can agree to not make any changes to the object, a fast path can be taken to streamline this process. This is achieved by wrapping the object with the Immutable class as shown in this example.

```
public async Task<Immutable<ExampleOutput>> DoSomething(Immutable<ExampleInput> input)
{
  var output = await DoSomething(input.Value);
  return output.AsImmutable();
}
```

An object can be wrapped by Immutable by calling the AsImmutable extension method. The Value property provides access to the object.

This optimization is only useful when grains are co-located, but the default behavior is that a new grains is created in the same Silos as its caller, so grains that cooperate will tend to live together.

External Tasks

Orleans uses a thread pool to schedule calls to grains. It's best practice not to starve this thread pool with CPU-intensive tasks. For CPU-intensive work, you may wish to consider a cloud-based serverless offering like Azure Functions or AWS Lambda.

It is possible to schedule tasks on .NET thread pool rather than the Orleans task scheduler; you just need to be careful about how you initiate a task.

When you use await, Task.Factory.StartNew, Task.ContinueWith, Task.WhenAny, Task.WhenAll, Task.Delay the current task scheduler is used, this means that the code will be executed in the scheduler used by the grains, and therefore observes the turn-based concurrency model. They can all be used inside grains.

When Task.Run is used, the task is executed on the .NET thread pool and escapes the grain's scheduler. This should only be used if you intentionally want to execute code outside of the grain's turn-based concurrency model for CPU-intensive workloads as discussed.

```
public async Task ExampleMethod()
{
  var task = Task.Run(() =>
  {
    // running outside the task scheduler
    // on the .NET thread pool
  });

  await task;
}
```

Controlling Grains Life Cycle

By default, Orleans will deactivate grains after a period of idleness (i.e., they have stopped receiving messages for two hours). But if we know we have finished with a grains, we can request immediate deactivation by calling DeactivateOnIdle. This is a method on the grains base class that can be called from within the grains.

This will deactivate after the current method call has completed. The next call to the grains will cause a new activation to be created.

If you want to alter the time to deactivation for a grains type, you can add the CollectionAgeLimit attribute to your grains class.

```
[CollectionAgeLimit(Minutes = 2)]
```

You can change the value at a Silos level by configuring the silos builder:

```
builder.Configure<GrainCollectionOptions>(x => x.CollectionAge =
TimeSpan.FromMinutes(2))
```

Summary

In this chapter, we cover a few features that can help to increase the performance of Orleans systems. Optimizations should be used carefully as most of them carry a side effect which you need to be mindful of.

CHAPTER 15

Advanced Features

In this chapter, we'll cover some of the advanced features available to the Orleans developer.

Request Context

RequestContext is a static class available within Grains which allows you to attach additional metadata to a request. The context then flows down to each grains in the call stack from where it can be read or updated.

This is useful when you have data like a correlation identifier that you need to pass through the system that isn't part of the main data model.

The request context includes a dictionary that allows you to add and remove values by a key, as well as an ActivityId property you can use for correlation.

```
// set a value
RequestContext.Set("correlation", Guid.NewGuid());

// get a value
var correlation = RequestContext.Get("correlation");

// remove a single entry
RequestContext.Remove("correlation");

// remove all entries
RequestContext.Clear();

// a convenience property you can use for correlation
RequestContext.ActivityId = Guid.NewGuid();

// enable propagation of CorrelationManager.ActivityId
RequestContext.PropagateActivityId = true;
```

© Richard Astbury 2022
R. Astbury, *Microsoft Orleans for Developers*, https://doi.org/10.1007/978-1-4842-8167-3_15

The request context is serialized when sent between Grains, so large data structures should be avoided.

The PropagateActivityId switch enables monitoring libraries that rely on CorrelationManager.ActivityId for correlation. For convenience, this can be enabled at a global level by configuring the silos builder:

```
hostBuilder.Configure<SiloMessagingOptions>(options =>
  options.PropagateActivityId = true);
```

Grains Call Filters

Grains call filters allow you to execute code before and after a method on a Grains is called. This can help with cross-cutting concerns such as authorization, logging, exception handling, and profiling. The Orleans Dashboard makes use of Grains Call Filters to count the number of a grains method calls, when they throw exceptions, and track the call duration.

There are two kinds of filters:

- **Incoming call filter**: Executed when a grains receives a call

- **Outgoing call filter**: Executed when a grains makes a call

Incoming Call Filters

To register an incoming call filter, you can use the AddIncomingGrainCallFilter extension method on the ISiloBuilder.

You can do this by providing a delegate; this example writes out the number of milliseconds each grains call took to execute:

```
builder.AddIncomingGrainCallFilter(async context =>
{
  var stopwatch = Stopwatch.StartNew();

  // call the grain method
  await context.Invoke();

  var time = stopwatch.ElapsedMilliseconds;
  var grainName = context.Grain.GetType().Name;
  var methodName = context.ImplementationMethod.Name;
  Console.WriteLine($"{grainName}.{methodName} = {time}ms");
})
```

Alternatively, you can implement `IIncomingGrainCallFilter` and register it using the same extension method:

`builder.AddIncomingGrainCallFilter<MyIncomingGrainCallFilter>()`

This has the advantage that you can access services using the constructor, including the grains client which you can use to make calls to other grains if required.

Note   If you wish to filter calls to just one specific grains type, you can do this by having the grains implement `IIncomingGrainCallFilter`.

The context argument contains several members that provide useful context to the call filter:

- **Arguments**: An array containing the values passed as arguments to the grains method.

- **InterfaceMethod**: The `MethodInfo` for the method declared on the grains interface.

- **ImplementationMethod**: The `MethodInfo` for the method on the grains.

- **Grains**: The identity of the grains.

- **Invoke**: The method on the grains, which should be called, unless you intentionally don't want to run the grain's method.

- **Result**: The value returned by the grains method. This will only be available once `Invoke()` has been awaited.

Grains call filters can also access the `RequestContext` static class to read/set metadata as described previously.

Outgoing Call Filters

Outgoing call filters are similar to their incoming counterparts. The difference is that they are executed when a call to a grains is made, rather than received. They do not carry the grains `MethodInfo` on the context object, just the `MethodInfo` for the interface.

To register an outgoing call filter, you can use the `AddOutgoingGrainCallFilter` extension method on the `ISiloBuilder`.

You can do this by providing a delegate; this example will write exceptions thrown when making a call:

```
builder.AddOutgoingGrainCallFilter(async x =>
{
  try
  {
    await x.Invoke();
  }
  catch (Exception ex)
  {
    Console.WriteLine(ex.ToString());
    throw;
  }
})
```

Alternatively, you can implement `IOutgoingGrainCallFilter` and register it with the same extension method. A grains can also inherit the interface, allowing you to intercept calls from one specific grains type.

Grains Placement

When a grains is activated, a placement director picks a Silos to host the Grains. This is a pluggable component responsible for selecting which Silos a grains should be activated in. There are five placement strategies provided that the Placement Director can be configured to use. You can also author your own. The default placement is random.

- **Random**: A random Silos is selected.

- **Local**: The local Silos is picked if it is compatible; otherwise, a random Silos is used.

- **Hash-Based**: The grain's identity is converted into an integer and then the modulo is calculated, using the number of Silos in the cluster. This value is then used to pick the Silos. This strategy means that grains pick consistent Silos until the cluster membership count changes.

- **Activation-Count-Based**: This strategy aims to balance the cluster by activating new grains in Silos that have fewer grains. Silos periodically publish their activation counts, which this placement director uses, along with the number of activations it has placed on each silos since the last update, to predict the number of grains on each Silos. To avoid situations where Silos with slightly fewer grains suddenly get overwhelmed, the placement director selects the top two (this number can be configured) candidate Silos and then randomly picks one of them.

- **StatelessWorker**: The placement strategy used by the stateless worker grains, described in the previous chapter, which is always activated in the same Silos as the caller, and can have multiple activations.

The default strategy is configured using dependency injection, by providing an implementation for the PlacementStrategy class.

```
builder.ConfigureServices(services =>
    services.AddSingleton<PlacementStrategy, RandomStrategy>());
```

You can override the default on a per-grains class using a custom attribute on the grains class.

```
[HashBasedPlacement]
public class MyGrain : Grain, IMyGrain
{
  ...
}
```

You can implement your own placement strategy, and I refer you to the documentation for details on how to accomplish that.

Startup Tasks

Sometimes we need to run some code in each Silos as part of a startup sequence. This code might initialize some required data and cache it, or start dequeuing messages from a queue to start feeding into Grains.

To achieve this, Orleans provides a way for us to register startup tasks using the `ISiloBuilder`. This can be implemented as a delegate:

```
builder.AddStartupTask(async (IServiceProvider services, CancellationToken
cancellation) =>
{
  var factory = services.GetRequiredService<IGrainFactory>();
  var grain = factory.GetGrain<IExampleGrain>();
  while(!cancellation.IsCancellationRequested)
  {
    grain.DoSomething();
    await Task.Delay(1000);
  }
})
```

The delegate is passed the `IServiceProvider`, allowing it to get a reference to the grains factory, allowing it to call grains. The cancellation token is cancelled when the Silos closes and indicates that the startup task should abort execution if it hasn't completed already.

Alternatively, you can implement the `IStartupTask` interface:

```
public interface IStartupTask
{
  Task Execute(CancellationToken cancellationToken);
}
```

Which can be registered in the `ISiloBuilder` using the same extension method:

```
builder.AddStartupTask<IStartupTask>()
```

Grains Service

A grains service is similar to a startup task, but instead of being a task, it's a Grains type that has a single activation per Silos. The Grains is kept active for the life of the Silos. As there is only ever one instance per Silos, the Grains does not have an identity.

Grains Services are useful for providing access to local resources on the Silos, such as accessing the disk, or for acting as a gateway to external services, such as receiving events from an event streaming subscription, and forwarding these on to Grains.

To create a Grains Service, first provide an interface that inherits IGrainService.

```
public interface IExampleGrainService: IGrainService
{
  Task DoSomething();
}
```

As with a normal Grains, you provide a concrete class that implements this interface. However, rather than inheriting Grain, you inherit GrainService.

```
public class ExampleGrainService : GrainService, IExampleGrainService
{
  public ExampleGrainService(
      IGrainIdentity id,
      Silo silo,
      ILoggerFactory loggerFactory)
      : base(id, silo, loggerFactory)
  { }
  public override Task Init(IServiceProvider serviceProvider)
  {
    Console.WriteLine("Init");
    return base.Init(serviceProvider);
  }
  public override Task Start()
  {
    Console.WriteLine("Start");
    return base.Start();
  }
  public override Task Stop()
  {
    Console.WriteLine("Stop");
    return base.Stop();
  }
```

```
  public Task DoSomething()
  {
    Console.WriteLine("DoSomething");
    return Task.CompletedTask;
  }
}
```

The GrainService base class provides a different set of virtual methods you can override for hooking into the grains life cycle. Instead of OnActivate and OnDeactivate, there are Init, Start, and Stop. Init is called first, providing the Grains Service with an IServiceProvider, which can be used to get a reference to the Grains Factory for calling Grains. The Init method allows you to complete any preparatory tasks required before the Silos is started. Start and Stop are then called when the respective events occur on the Silos.

Note   A Grains Service cannot write directly to an Orleans Stream. Instead, the Grains Service should call a regular grains which can in turn write to the stream.

The Grains Service can be registered with the Silos using the AddGrainService extension method on ISiloBuilder. Unless a client is also defined (as explained in the following), the Grains Service must also be registered as a service.

```
builder
  .AddGrainService<ExampleGrainService>()
  .ConfigureServices(s =>
  {
s.AddSingleton<IExampleGrainService,ExampleGrainService>();
  })
```

The Grains Service can be called from other grains, although there are a few steps required to create a client class to do so.

First create an interface that represents the client. This inherits IGrainServiceClient<T>, where T is the interface for the Grains Service. It also inherits the Grains Service interface directly:

```
public interface IExampleGrainServiceClient :
  IGrainServiceClient<IExampleGrainService>,
  IExampleGrainService
{ }
```

To create the client class, inherit `GrainServiceClient<T>`, where T is the interface for the Grains Service. This class should also inherit the previously defined interface for the Grains Service Client.

```
public class ExampleGrainServiceClient :
  GrainServiceClient<IExampleGrainService>,
  IExampleGrainServiceClient
{
  public GrainServiceClient(IServiceProvider serviceProvider)
      : base(serviceProvider)
  { }

  public Task DoSomething() => this.GrainService.DoSomething();
}
```

The class needs to provide mappings between the methods defined on the Grains Service interface and the methods on the inherited `GrainService` property. In this case, we map the `DoSomething` method.

The client can then be registered as a service:

```
builder.ConfigureServices(s =>
{
  s.AddSingleton<
    IExampleGrainServiceClient, ExampleGrainServiceClient>();
})
```

The `IExampleGrainServiceClient` can then be added as a parameter on the constructor of a Grains, allowing it to make calls to the Grains Service.

```
public class ExampleGrain : Grain, IExampleGrain
{
  private IExampleGrainServiceClient client;
```

```
public ExampleGrain(IExampleGrainServiceClient client)
{
  this.client = client;
}

public override async Task OnActivateAsync()
{
  // call the grain service on activate
  await this.client.DoSomething();
  await base.OnActivateAsync();
}
}
```

Observers

An observer provides a mechanism for a grains to call back to a client. In many scenarios, a stream may be better suited, but an Observer is a lighter-weight alternative that provides a best-effort delivery without an underlying pub-sub system.

Observers are one-way messages, and similar to one-way requests, the caller does not know if the message was delivered successfully. You should therefore only consider observers for messages that can be lost, or you include a separate return channel to ensure delivery was successful.

To create an observer, first create an interface to define the methods that you want to be called.

```
public interface IProgressObserver : IGrainObserver
{
  void UpdateProgress(int value);
}
```

The interface must implement IGrainObserver.

Observers only provide one-way messaging, so unlike methods on Grains that return a Task, the methods on an observer cannot have a return value and must be void.

It is the responsibility of the grains to maintain the list of observers and to call them at the appropriate time. We would therefore expect to see methods on the grains for adding and removing observers.

The interface would look like this:

```
public interface IExampleGrain : IGrainWithStringKey
{
  Task Subscribe(IProgressObserver observer);
  Task Unsubscribe(IProgressObserver observer);
  Task DoSomething();
}
```

A naïve implementation of the grains would look like this:

```
public class ExampleGrain : Grain, IExampleGrain
{
  List<IProgressObserver> observers =
    new List<IProgressObserver>();

  public Task Subscribe(IProgressObserver observer)
  {
    this.observers.Add(observer);
    return Task.CompletedTask;
  }

  public Task Unsubscribe(IProgressObserver observer)
  {
    this.observers.Remove(observer);
    return Task.CompletedTask;
  }

  void Notify(int value)
  {
    this.observers.ForEach(x =>
      x.UpdateProgress(value));
  }

  public async Task DoSomething()
  {
    for (var i = 0; i <= 100; i += 10)
    {
      this.Notify(i);
```

```
        await Task.Delay(1000);
    }
  }
}
```

The grains maintains its observers, using the Subscribe and Unsubscribe methods to add or remove observer references from a list. To notify an observer, it simply calls the relevant method.

This example is oversimplified. It's not possible for the grains to know if the observer object still exists in the client process. Stale observers may also throw an exception, which should be handled and the observer reference removed.

It is recommended practice to set a timeout for observers and automatically remove them unless they are re-registered.

In Orleans version 4, we hope to see a utility class to help observer management easier.

To implement the observer in the client, we need to provide a concrete class that implements our interface:

```
public class ProgressObserver : IProgressObserver
{
  public void UpdateProgress(int value)
  {
    Console.WriteLine($"{value}% complete");
  }
}
```

Before we can call the Subscribe method on the grains, we must first create an instance of the observer and then create a reference of it. It's the reference that is passed to the grains, rather than our concrete class. The CreateObjectReference method on the grains client creates this reference for us.

```
var observer = await client
  .CreateObjectReference<IProgressObserver>(
    new ProgressObserver());

var grain = client.GetGrain<IExampleGrain>(grainId);
await grain.Subscribe(observer);
await grain.DoSomething();
```

The `CreateObjectReference` method returns an observer with a weak reference. To avoid this from being garbage collected, you should hold on to your own reference of the observer by making it a member of your grains.

When running this code, we see the observer in the client application being called when the notify method executes in the grains.

Grains can also be observers; the Grains just needs to implement `IExampleObserver`. It is not necessary to use `CreateObjectReference` to create the reference to the Grains; instead, you just use `AsReference<T>` extension method.

The code a grains would use to register itself as an observer with the example grains would look like this:

```
var exampleGrain = this.GrainFactory
  .GetGrain<IExampleGrain>("x");

var grainReference = this.AsReference<IProgressObserver>();
await exampleGrain.Subscribe(grainReference);
await exampleGrain.DoSomething();
```

Given that a grains can call another back directly, without the use of observers, makes this approach less useful than calling back a client.

CHAPTER 16

Interviews

I believe that when you are using a technology or platform, it is always helpful to have some understanding or insight into how it came into being.

In this final chapter of the book, I thought it might be both interesting and useful for me to share some interviews that introduce you both to the people involved in the creation of Orleans and a CTO who began using Orleans almost from its inception.

Roger Creyke

Roger is the founder and CTO of a big data streaming analytics startup in the sports betting industry. He has a long history of working with Orleans, including on key business-critical systems for multinational sports betting companies, and was one of the first non-Microsoft users of the system. He has some great insights into working with Orleans and building high-scale distributed applications that process large data volumes at speed.

When did you first decide to use Orleans?

Engineers at my studio at the time investigated technologies which could help us with the processing and redistribution of sports betting price data at high scale. They came back with a number of technologies, including the 2014 research paper on Orleans, which I found fascinating.

The *Halo 4* stats service had been running the tech for a number of years already (they had internal access to Orleans via the Microsoft Research incubator as part of Microsoft Game Studios), so that built some confidence in its maturity, despite a lack of public information.

© Richard Astbury 2022
R. Astbury, *Microsoft Orleans for Developers*, https://doi.org/10.1007/978-1-4842-8167-3_16

I visited the Orleans team when they were co-located with the *Halo* team at 343 Industries in a basement in Redmond, Washington. 343 were using the framework to process huge amounts of telemetry data from millions of multiplayer games. We discussed whether the framework would also suit the demands of our globally distributed sports betting platform and I pitched a collaboration where in turn we would help to validate a new feature that they had a postdoc working on.

Other than the *Halo* workload, my confidence in the project was also bolstered by the enthusiasm and competence of the project lead Sergey Bykov (who is now putting the experience to good use at Temporal.io), as well having Phil Bernstein (a Distinguished Engineer at Microsoft) advising the team.

By the time I left, I felt it was likely to be successfully adopted by the community, could solve our business challenges, and would likely continue to be supported for the foreseeable future.

Why Orleans?

The team were competent .NET developers, but we needed to scale up the tech while holding a lot of state in memory so actors seemed a good option. We looked at Akka.NET and Orleans, and while Akka.NET was impressive, Orleans won for us as it was designed with .NET asynchronous tasks in mind and the first class citizen clustering ensured location transparency with minimal opt-in cluster orchestration.

State, durability, fault tolerance, partitioning of data and compute, and data locality were really important. Getting the code as close to the data (in memory) meant we could react faster and make quicker decisions. There are tens of thousands of significant sporting events every day, and we couldn't drop messages.

How would you build something without an actor framework?

I wouldn't scream about it. Actors and virtual actors are a great architectural tool, and if you build nontrivial services, I highly recommend adding them to your box of tricks, but I am not an extremist and I am happy to build systems in a more mainstream way using a combination of hand-rolled or open source read-through caching, stateless stream processing, and technologies such as Apache Spark and Apache Flink.

You're currently using Orleans in production; could you describe your architecture?

We dynamically converge streams of pricing, wagering, and real-time positional and game event data from thousands of sporting events a day to perform real-time and retrospective analytics. Orleans grains eat through Kafka events and keep track of state, and when trigger conditions are met, output metrics and alerts. We run Orleans in Kubernetes, and our overall deployment is a healthy mixture of serverless and containers.

How easy is Orleans to manage?

It's a powerful framework designed for some of the most demanding services, so while the configurability is high, that does mean there is a bit of domain knowledge to pick up and run a big cluster. Rolling out new code while the system is running and is holding live state as grains contracts change can be challenging, but there is great community tooling around this, and plenty of support. Developing polyglot persistence storage-backed applications and running hybrid cloud scenarios where different storage providers are used per deployment is an incredibly productive experience as the application code rarely interacts with storage directly.

Over the years, you've picked Orleans for several projects; what keeps bringing you back?

I work on a lot of real-time big data stream processing systems. Once you model these kinds of systems with actors, it becomes a much more natural way to rationalize about them. Event processing often requires state, and it's easier to work with state in lots of small pieces (one actor per state collection). Orleans also makes dealing with race conditions as grains sit within a single-threaded execution model and can't (unless explicitly requested) handle multiple requests in parallel. The framework is incredibly extensible; you can plug in different storage, streaming, and telemetry providers so that also keeps me coming back.

What do you see as Orleans' greatest strengths/ weaknesses?

The community is a huge strength. Because it's small and full of distributed systems experts and academics, there's no lack of support or solutions to a problem. Because Orleans has less mouths to feed than ASP.NET, the development team can communicate directly with customers.

Because Orleans was designed to cluster natively, it is very quick to get up and running and then scale up later without making code changes.

What would you change about Orleans?

I'd actually rename it to ASP.NET Grains and sell it as an add-on to supercharge ASP.NET rather than a distributed compute framework that can optionally handle requests from a Web API. Messaging matters, and while it papers over the complexity to call it that, it would drive wider adoption, especially if a cloud offering was to be offered alongside it. The power users can create clusters without Web APIs, but I'm confident the majority would just add the distributed caching, streaming, messaging, and stateful scaling to their API and be super happy.

Why do you think Orleans isn't more popular?

While many product teams can benefit from the virtual actor model, the majority of those can suboptimally struggle on without it. This isn't a good reason to dismiss technologies like Orleans, but it can go some way to explain the lack of mainstream adoption. If necessity is the mother of invention, then ignorance is justifiable without her.

A combination of quite loosely related business requirements such as scaling, availability, message throughput, low latency, and stateful stream processing can compound to a point where it is deemed appropriate to find an unorthodox technology which helps tackle these at the framework level, but it takes a good mix of those to go off the well-worn track.

The virtual actor concept also requires a bit of brain rewiring. Holding state in memory and not ensuring thread safety when accessing shared state have long been treated as a bad idea.

Messaging is everything. Why should I learn this new technology? How can it benefit me and my team? What amazing products have been supported by it? What are the common use cases in key industries which would likely benefit from it? It's a big turning circle to convince traditional shops to go all-in on a new application framework and shun the industry norms of stateless APIs and microservices with their own databases. What the relationship is between Orleans and ASP.NET, for example, is not something clear to new users.

Sergey Bykov

Sergey Bykov led the Orleans team from the beginning taking an internal research project, to a critical part of infrastructure to support *Halo* and *Gears of War*, to a popular open source project and member of the dotnet foundation. Sergey is now at Temporal, a startup building an open source orchestration engine, leading their Temporal Cloud project.

Where did the name for Orleans come from?

Microsoft has a long tradition of using names of cities as codenames. The reason for that is trivial – such names cannot be copyrighted, and therefore the company cannot be sued by a copyright holder. When I came to Microsoft Research to work on the project, the name was already chosen. So, I'm not actually 100% certain how exactly it came about.

What was it like to take an internal research project and publish it as open source?

That was a pivotal point for the project. On the one hand, it was still a vibrant research project, with a bunch of further ideas to explore. On the other hand, it was already a product with several years of production use. The decision was made to "graduate" it from research and go the product route. We believed that open source was the only good path to take even though those were the early days of Microsoft's turn to it. It was exciting to be working completely in the open, directly interacting with the global community of smart and motivated people, to have those people tell us what is good and what's not, and to contribute their ideas into the project. At the time, Microsoft had a reputation of sometimes cancelling projects that it heavily promoted just a few years prior to that. Open source is the best insurance for users of a project that it won't disappear one day.

A few months before then, Microsoft open sourced the .NET runtime and framework. Talking to their engineers helped us to avoid some basic mistakes and set up the processes right from the start. But we also got infected by the open source enthusiasm that the .NET team was radiating.

We managed to maintain our connection with Microsoft Research and, over time, successfully collaborated with them on several projects.

What benefits did you see from open sourcing Orleans?

I already mentioned some of the benefits. Open source keeps you as a developer honest. Developers tell you they don't like right away. If you listen, ask clarifying questions, and stay open-minded, the project gets better in ways it wouldn't if it stayed proprietary. I remember we had code-generated factory classes in the original release. We were immediately told that it was a bad pattern. We yanked them right away and embraced a better approach.

What I enjoyed the most was the community that quickly formed around Orleans. Smart motivated engineers that are also very nice individuals, always ready to help each other and answer questions from beginners. I became friends with several people through the community. I loved our virtual meetups (that you organized) where people from around the world would join to present their work and ideas.

The community not only contributed their code, fixes, and feedback; the whole contrib organization has been created on GitHub and populated with various extension projects. Orleans Dashboard is the prime example of a contrib project that became a staple component for most people using Orleans.

Were there any use cases for Orleans that took you by surprise?

One of my first major surprises was when we organized a private hackathon with seven companies that were early adopters of Orleans. Three of them ended up building various forms of workflows for automating business processes. I didn't expect that at all, but the basic features of persistent state and reminders were enough for them to do that.

Another interesting use case was when Gutemberg Ribeiro from the Orleans community rewrote the entire back end of the payment processing product of his company over a weekend. Two weeks later, they were running in production.

The most exciting to me was the project by Mesh Systems and Steffes of managing in real time·ceramic water heaters as inexpensive thermal "batteries" for storing excessive renewable energy on the island of Oahu (`https://meshsystems.com/assets/Files/Mesh-Systems-Steffes-Corporation-IoT-Story-1.pdf`).

Where do development teams get the most value from using Orleans?

I think the most value comes from the basics – the ability to build software using objects, grains, that live in the virtual "address space" of a cluster of machines as if they were in a single process. Fortunately, development of Orleans coincided with the adoption of asynchronous programming and the primitives for it, tasks and await. By the time we went open source, it was much easier to sell people on the idea of grains interfaces with asynchronous methods and writing non-blocking code. Being able to call grains via their stable identities without worrying about their life cycle greatly simplified many scenarios where the state of the application is naturally partitioned. This was a great fit for sessions, accounts, gaming, IoT, and other domains where Orleans enjoyed good adoption.

You have moved on from Orleans now, but where do you see the future of cloud-native applications going?

As they say, it's difficult to make predictions, especially about the future. I can think of several possibilities that may play out in parallel. It's clear to me that the virtual actor model pioneered by Orleans is here to stay. It has already been adopted to different degrees in multiple products and is growing in popularity. Cross-language interoperability with language-specific extensions could make the idea of cloud-native objects a reality. Cloud hosting offerings for such objects would reduce the operational overhead of running applications and services built with them. WASM is intriguing from the security and determinism perspective. Adding reliably executing workflows as an off-the-shelf primitive for business logic and long-running processes should empower developers even further. That's where my focus is these days.

But to be honest, I have no real idea where cloud-native applications are going. Our industry is full of surprises. We'll see. That's part of the joy of our profession.

Index

© Richard Astbury 2022
R. Astbury, *Microsoft Orleans for Developers*, https://doi.org/10.1007/978-1-4842-8167-3

V

W, X, Y, Z

Printed in the United States
by Baker & Taylor Publisher Services